Success Secrets of Rich, Smart and Powerful People:

How You Can Use Leverage for Business Success

2nd Edition, significantly modified

Tom Marcoux
America's Communication Coach
TFG Thought Leader
Speaker-Author of 25 books
Blogger, BeHeardandBeTrusted.com

A QuickBreakthrough Publishing Edition

ISBN: 0692358501
ISBN-13: 978-0692358504

QuickBreakthrough Publishing is an imprint of Tom Marcoux Media, LLC. More copies are available from the publisher, Tom Marcoux Media, LLC. Please call (415) 572-6609 or write TomSuperCoach@gmail.com
or visit www.TomSuperCoach.com
or Tom's blog: www.BeHeardandBeTrusted.com
This book was developed and written with care. Names and details were modified to respect privacy.

Disclaimer: The author and publisher acknowledge that each person's situation is unique, and that readers have full responsibility to seek consultations with health, financial, spiritual and legal professionals. The author and publisher make no representations or warranties of any kind, and the author and publisher shall not be liable for any special, consequential or exemplary damages resulting, in whole or in part, from the reader's use of, or reliance upon, this material.:

Other Books by Tom Marcoux:

- Be Heard and Be Trusted: How to Get What You Want
- Nothing Can Stop You This Year!
- Reduce Clutter, Enlarge Your Life
- Darkest Secrets of Persuasion and Seduction Masters
- Darkest Secrets of Charisma
- Darkest Secrets of Negotiation Masters
- Darkest Secrets of the Film and Television Industry Every Actor Should Know
- Darkest Secrets of Making a Pitch to the Film and Television Industry
- Darkest Secrets of Film Directing
- Truth No One Will Tell You

Praise for *Success Secrets of Rich, Smart and Powerful People* and Tom Marcoux

• "This book is both powerful and unique. It's not the usual marketing book that is simply an encyclopedia of tips. Instead, it gives you an Action Plan and 9-minute Methods that get you moving. This is the only marketing book I know of that helps you overcome procrastination, in addition to helping you effectively position your product or service for your target market. If you have any uncertainty about your positioning and target market or your next marketing step . . . get this book!"
– Danek S. Kaus, author of *You Can Be Famous! Insider Secrets to Getting Free Publicity*

• "Get Tom Marcoux's *Success Secrets of Rich, Smart and Powerful People.* I repeatedly hire Tom Marcoux as my media coach. He works on my press releases and consults on the covers of my books. I trust Tom's instincts the most. I value his opinions and ideas so much. He really has a good eye for marketing." – Dr. JoAnn Dahlkoetter, Coach to Olympic Gold Medalists and CEOs and author of *Your Performing Edge*

Praise for Tom Marcoux's Other Work:

• "In *Reduce Clutter, Enlarge Your Life*, Marcoux will help you get rid of the physical and mental clutter occupying precious space in your life. You'll reclaim wasted energy, lower your stress, and find time for new opportunities." – Laura Stack, author of *Execution IS the Strategy*

• "In *Power Time Management*, Tom Marcoux shares his extraordinary strategies and methods that save you time, make you money and increase your success and happiness. As Tom's client for many years, I have benefited from his wisdom and strategic approach. Do your career and personal life a big favor and get this book." – Dr. JoAnn Dahlkoetter, author, *Your Performing Edge* and to CEOs & Olympic Gold Medalists

• "In *Darkest Secrets of Persuasion and Seduction Masters*, learn useful countermeasures to protect yourself from being darkly manipulated."
– David Barron, co-author, *Power Persuasion*

• "In *Be Heard and Be Trusted*, Tom's advice on how to remain true to yourself and establish authentic rapport with clients is both insightful and reality based. He [shows how] to establish oneself as a credible expert."
-Arthur P. Ciaramicoli, Ed.D., Ph.D., author *The Curse of the Capable*

Visit Tom's blog: www.BeHeardandBeTrusted.com

CONTENTS

DEDICATION AND ACKNOWLEDGEMENTS

This book is dedicated to the terrific book and film consultant, and author Johanna E. Mac Leod. It is also dedicated to the other team members.

Thanks for 24 guest articles by guest authors Brian Tracy, Patricia Fripp, Chip Conley, Mark Sanborn, Dr. Elayne Savage, Dr. Tony Alessandra, Noah St. John, Jeanna Gabellini, C.J. Hayden, Willie Jolley, Linda Finkle, Gayl Murphy, Paul Gillin, Linda L. Chappo, John S. Rhodes, David, Garfinkel, Beth Barany, Ezra Barany, Lois Creamer, Judi Moreo, Elaine Fogel, Stephanie Beeby, Kimberly Gleason, and Danek S. Kaus [Their articles remain with their original copyright and are included in this book by their permission.]

Thanks to David MacDowell Blue, Danek S. Kaus, Sherry Lusk and Joan Harrison for editing. Thanks to my father, Al Marcoux, for his concern and efforts for me. Thanks to my mother, Sumiyo Marcoux, a kind, generous soul. Thanks to Johanna E. Mac Leod for rendering this book's cover. Thank you to Higher Power and our enthusiastic audiences and readers. The best to you.

Success Secrets of Rich, Smart and Powerful People – (plus Your Countermeasures and 9-minute Methods)

Several years ago, I sent a book proposal to a book agent. Within sixty minutes of receiving my FedEx package, he called.

Ultimately, this agent passed on representing my book to publishers, saying it was too similar to other book projects. But I noticed something. He didn't talk much about the book itself. Instead, he concentrated on the marketing section of my proposal.

Upon reflection, I realized why he passed. I was missing something: *Leverage!*

That was *before* I had a popular blog at www.BeHeardandBeTrusted.com, thousands of contacts at Linkedin.com, Facebook, Twitter, Google+, and 25 books published. Also before I taught MBA students at Stanford University and more. These elements *indicate leverage and influence.*

You see agents and publishers want to know that an author has the leverage to sell lots of books.

How about you? What do you really want? I can assure you that leverage can be the key to getting what you want and faster than you expected.

This book helps you gain access to the wisdom of rich, smart and powerful people. Why? I want you to have leverage to make your dreams come true. Merriam-Webster.com defines *leverage* as "influence or power used to achieve a desired result" and "the increase in force gained by using a lever."

This second element grabs my attention. Using a lever, one can move a boulder with little effort. But more than that, it's about increasing personal power to get what you want. Ten individuals using their own personal strength can move that bolder. One individual with the right tool can move that bolder using less strength than if he or she was part of a large team.

We're not talking about boulders. We're talking about whatever you want—your ambitions, your hopes.

It's all about building that lever. A primary building block is the knowledge, advice and warnings of people who've accomplished what you want to accomplish.

This book functions as your lever to business success.

When I sent out that proposal, I didn't have any books published. I now have over twenty-five books published.

Along the way I sought numerous mentors and have trained with a number of successful people to hone daily practices that create leverage.

I've distilled this into what I call the L.I.F.T. process of leverage.

L - listen
I - increase networking
F - focus on "help them first"
T - team up

1. Listen

Do you want to get people to like you and trust you quickly? When that happens, your personal leverage to get things done increases exponentially. The answer: *Learn to listen well.* Here are three methods:

A – attend
R – reflect
E – engage emotions

a. Attend

Give your full attention. Make sure that your heart faces their heart ("Heart faces heart.")

At times, I begin a conversation with, "I'm listening. What would you like me to know about the situation?" The reason for this beginning is sometimes the situation may have some heat to it. When I listen first, the tension drains from the situation.

Think about it: How often does one get fully listened to? Can you imagine what a relief it is to have your thoughts and feelings heard without interruption or automatic judgment?

Near the end of a conversation, I ask, "Is there anything else you need me to know?" Again, this is about giving full attention.

b. Reflect

Provide what I call "Reflective Replies." Reflect their concerns and emotions. Say things like: "That sounds frustrating" or "That sounds hard to endure."

Why is this valuable?

First, we often do not know if someone understands the meaning behind our words. Reflective Replies assure the speaker that you understand the meaning. Or if you say something a bit off, the speaker can use other words to clarify his or her meaning.

Second, you do NOT tell another person what they are feeling. You provide a gentle phrase: "That sounds . . ."

For example, you might say, "That sounds frustrating."

But the person says, "Not frustrating, disappointing."

You can ask, "What disappointed you the most about this situation?" That question signals that you are being fully present with the person in the moment.

c. Engage emotions

Help the person feel it is safe to share their feelings. Someone may say, "That driver made me mad." Often, I'll reply, "Okay." For me "okay" is neutral. I do not have to agree. By saying "okay" I'm communicating, "I'm hearing you. It's okay to feel whatever you're feeling."

I have an elderly relative who has horrible habits when it comes to listening. This guy only pauses between things he wants to say. It does not feel safe to express a feeling around him. I have actually said, "You cannot logic me out of my feelings. I get to feel the way I feel about this."

Instead, as a good listener, you make a safe place for the other person to express his or her feelings. Once a person feels heard, often the energy about a situation "cools off."

Listening well is a big part of creating success and fulfillment in our lives. How do you get loyalty and reliable efforts from other people? Listen to them well.

Start practicing today.

You'll discover how your business and personal relationships improve.

2. Increase networking

You will do better when people look upon you as a "hub of influence." You can start by aiming to increase the number of your Linkedin.com contacts to over 500. When you get "500+" added to your Linkedin.com profile you look well-connected and like a *mover-and-shaker.*

Here are three tips:

a) Thank people. If you see a well-done article, video, or slide show, share it with others. Then send a thank you message or card to the author(s). Let them know who is benefiting from their good work. After they respond, send an invitation to connect at Linkedin.com.

b) Increase your visibility. Write a blog. If you're not a wordsmith, post articles by guest-bloggers. One of my editors asked, "How does this help you if you're just showing off others' work?" I replied, "You become known as the Founder of ____ blog and as a well-connected professional."

c) Give a presentation. When you meet someone in an audience at a conference, you meet as peers. On the other hand, give a presentation and you gain instant credibility as an expert. Ask for my free report "9 Deadly Mistakes to Avoid for Your Next Speech and 9 Surefire Methods" at http://tomsupercoach.com/freereport9Mistakes4Speech.html

3. Focus on "help them first"

I share with my clients and graduate students something I call *The 3 Magic Words of Networking.* They are: *Help Them First.*

Develop business friendships. You could help someone by simply being a good listener upon meeting them at a networking event, for example.

Ask people, "How can I be supportive of what you're doing?"

In order to ask that question with more ease, learn how to say no gracefully. For example, I do charitable work and make contributions. And there are times when someone invites me to donate to their charity. First, I get something I call thinkspace—time and space to think through a proposal. I reply with something like: "I'll need to look at some budgets here. How about I get back to you on Thursday afternoon?"

If I'm not drawn to the particular cause, I sometimes reply, "Thanks for thinking of me. I'm sad to report that my funds are pre-committed in another direction."

I have advised clients to avoid the phrase, "I can't afford it" because it is such a personal energy-draining comment.

Whenever you say, something that begins with "I"—in essence you're programming yourself on the subconscious level. That's why I emphasize the comment: "My funds are pre-committed in another direction."

My overall point is that master-networkers ask people how they can be supportive of them. And such master-networkers avoid being afraid of the question because they know they can say *no* gracefully.

4. Team up

Nothing is impossible for the man who doesn't have to do it himself. – A. H. Weiler

Consider teaming up.

Every project I complete is a team effort. I work hard to be supportive of friends, acquaintances and team members. In return, I'm grateful for a lot of support.

For example, I asked a friend to give me a quick reaction to a potential book title for material I was working on. She gave me insight about the book title. How great! She was on my team for two precious minutes. The truth is: I'm on *her* team. She's a part of my circle.

For longer interactions, clearly communicate some benefits the person will *personally* receive. Sometimes, we have a misguided thought that if we provide a benefit for someone's work group or company, then the individual will feel good about it. However, it's better to make sure that the individual you're speaking with receives some form of *personal* benefit.

There's a wide world out there. You can team up with so many people. Whether it's two minutes to send a link about a temporary employment agency to a jobseeker or twenty minutes to hear a friend's concerns about a family member, listen up and team up.

With an extensive network, you have *more leverage.*

* * * * * *

Leverage Focus Points of Rich, Smart and Powerful People

Rich, smart and powerful people do certain things repeatedly. As author Randy Gage emphasizes: rich people do things that other people do not do.

If you want to be rich, you cannot be normal. - Noah St. John

I've learned that making things memorable is often more important that providing a huge list or a big book (I've written some books at 390 pages and 470 pages).

So for maximum impact, I have organized the advice of rich, smart and powerful people under **10 Leverage Focus Points.**

Leverage Focus Point #1: Listen

Success is a lousy teacher. It seduces smart people into thinking they can't lose. - Bill Gates

Your most unhappy customers are your greatest source of learning. - Bill Gates

* * * * * *

Leverage Focus Point #2: Lead

Someone's sitting in the shade today because someone planted a tree a long time ago. - Warren Buffett

Decision making is easy if your values are clear.
- Roy O. Disney

As we look ahead into the next century, leaders will be those who empower others. - Bill Gates

The first rule of any technology used in a business is that automation applied to an efficient operation will magnify the efficiency. The second is that automation applied to an inefficient operation will magnify the inefficiency.
- Bill Gates

To solve any problem, here are three questions to ask yourself: First, what could I do? Second, what could I read? And third, who could I ask? - Jim Rohn

Leaders think and talk about the solutions. Followers think and talk about the problems. - Brian Tracy

Successful people are always looking for opportunities to help others. Unsuccessful people are always asking, "What's in it for me?" - Brian Tracy

Winners make a habit of manufacturing their own positive expectations in advance of the event. - Brian Tracy

Leaders must be close enough to relate to others, but far enough ahead to motivate them. - John C. Maxwell

If you set out to be liked, you would be prepared to compromise on anything at any time, and you would achieve nothing. - Prime Minister Margaret Thatcher

You may have to fight a battle more than once to win it.
- Prime Minister Margaret Thatcher

The art of leadership is saying no, not saying yes. It is very easy to say yes. - Prime Minister Tony Blair

If you're going through hell, keep going.
- Prime Minister Winston Churchill

Courage is what it takes to stand up and speak; courage is also what it takes to sit down and listen.
- Prime Minister Winston Churchill

* * * * * *

Leverage Focus Point #3: Learn

I really had a lot of dreams when I was a kid, and I think a great deal of that grew out of the fact that I had a chance to read a lot. - Bill Gates

Leadership and learning are indispensable to each other.
- President John F. Kennedy

Leverage Focus Point #4: Listen to Intuition and Think

It takes 20 years to build a reputation and five minutes to ruin it. If you think about that, you'll do things differently.
- Warren Buffett

It is a universal principle that you get more of what you think about, talk about, and feel strongly about.
- Jack Canfield

A public-opinion poll is no substitute for thought.
- Warren Buffett

The business schools reward difficult complex behavior more than simple behavior, but simple behavior is more effective. - Warren Buffett

Risk comes from not knowing what you're doing.
- Warren Buffett

Sometimes when people are under stress, they hate to think, and it's the time when they most need to think.
- President William J. Clinton

* * * * * *

Leverage Focus Point #5: Consider Information

from People Who Have Accomplished What You Want to Accomplish

Wall Street is the only place that people ride to in a Rolls Royce to get advice from those who take the subway.
- Warren Buffett

(Another way to say this is: Some rich people get advice from certain stock brokers who lack necessary knowledge.)

* * * * * *

Leverage Focus Point #6: Choose Your Companions With Great Care

It's better to hang out with people better than you. Pick out associates whose behavior is better than yours and you'll drift in that direction. - Warren Buffett

Surround yourself with only people who are going to lift you higher. - Oprah Winfrey

Lots of people want to ride with you in the limo, but what you want is someone who will take the bus with you when the limo breaks down. - Oprah Winfrey

Of the billionaires I have known, money just brings out the basic traits in them. If they were jerks before they had money, they are simply jerks with a billion dollars.
- Warren Buffett

* * * * * *

Leverage Focus Point #7: Be Courageous and Take Action

Think like a queen. A queen is not afraid to fail. Failure is another steppingstone to greatness. - Oprah Winfrey

I believe that every single event in life happens is an opportunity to choose love over fear. - Oprah Winfrey

Change will not come if we wait for some other person or some other time. We are the ones we've been waiting for. We are the change that we seek. - President Barack Obama

The future rewards those who press on. I don't have time to feel sorry for myself. I don't have time to complain. I'm going to press on. - President Barack Obama

You cannot escape the responsibility of tomorrow by evading it today. - President Abraham Lincoln

I will do what others will not do so in the future I can do what others cannot do. - Randy Gage

* * * * * *

Leverage Focus Point #8: Do the Best You Can with What You Have in This Moment

My philosophy is that not only are you responsible for your life, but doing the best at this moment puts you in the best place for the next moment.
- Oprah Winfrey

You just have to keep trying to do good work, and hope that it leads to more good work. I want to look back on my career and be proud of the work, and be proud that I tried everything. - Jon Stewart

* * * * * *

Leverage Focus Point #9: Cultivate an Empowering Mindset

Be thankful for what you have; you'll end up having more. If you concentrate on what you don't have, you will never, ever have enough. - Oprah Winfrey

I am a woman in process. I'm just trying like everybody else. I try to take every conflict, every experience, and learn from it. Life is never dull. - Oprah Winfrey

We can't help everyone, but everyone can help someone.
- President Ronald Reagan

I always knew I was going to be rich. I don't think I ever doubted it for a minute. - Warren Buffett

Strength and wisdom are not opposing values.
- President William J. Clinton

Always bear in mind that your own resolution to succeed is more important than any other.
- President Abraham Lincoln

I've found that luck is quite predictable. If you want more luck, take more chances. Be more active. Show up more often. - Brian Tracy

When your self-worth goes up, your net worth goes up with it. - Mark Victor Hansen

Whoever renders service to many puts himself in line for greatness—great wealth, great return, great satisfaction, great reputation, and great joy. - Jim Rohn

We make a living by what we get, but we make a life by what we give. - Winston Churchill

You are not here merely to make a living. You are here in order to enable the world to live more amply, with greater vision, with a finer spirit of hope and achievement. You are here to enrich the world, and you impoverish yourself if you forget the errand. - President Woodrow Wilson

Success is not the key to happiness. Happiness is the key to success. If you love what you are doing, you will be successful. - Albert Schweitzer

We must all suffer from one of two pains: the pain of discipline or the pain of regret. The difference is discipline weighs ounces while regret weighs tons. - Jim Rohn

* * * * * *

Leverage Focus Point #10: Prepare Well

Give me six hours to chop down a tree and I will spend the first four sharpening the axe. - President Abraham Lincoln

I do not think much of a man who is not wiser today than he was yesterday. - President Abraham Lincoln

* * *

Here is a summary:

10 Leverage Focus Points of Rich, Smart and Powerful People

1. Listen
2. Lead
3. Learn
4. Listen to Intuition and Think
5. Consider Information from People Who Have Accomplished What You Want to Accomplish
6. Choose Your Companions with Great Care
7. Be Courageous and Take Action
8. Do the Best You Can with What You Have in This Moment
9. Cultivate an Empowering Mindset
10. Prepare Well.

In closing this section, I'll add my comment:

Do something today. It's "Better than zero." - Tom Marcoux

* * * * * *

Rich, Smart and Powerful People Use Leverage in Two Crucial Areas: Overcoming Procrastination and Marketing.

What's a dirty word in small business marketing? *Procrastination.* Waiting too long. Waiting until it's too late. Finding an excuse to do something, *anything,* other than what needs doing right now. Many of us procrastinate as a habit. And such behavior can deny you everything that you've earned. It throws sand in the gears of your life, and it crushes your dreams. Yet almost everyone does it.

Many books provide marketing tips. What makes this book different and especially useful is that it faces the reality about procrastination. You must become skilled in overcoming this habit and then doing the *effective things* that market your business (or yourself if you're a freelancer).

Before we go further, let's celebrate that *you probably started your business because you like helping people and that you're really good at doing something* that can bring benefits into people's lives. Congratulations!

And for many of us, marketing is that mountain that we must climb over to get back to doing what we're good at—the core of our business.

What is marketing? *The Merriam-Webster Dictionary* defines *marketing* as "The act or process of selling or purchasing in a market . . . The process or technique of promoting, selling, and distributing a product or service . . . An aggregate of functions involved in moving goods from producer to consumer."

What is *effective* marketing? **First, it is marketing that you actually do**. Second, it is efficient and targeted efforts. We'll cover both of those steps in this book. You'll use vital *9-minute Methods* to get started quickly.

Let's get going.

Secret #1: Many of us resist marketing.

Marketing remains the lifeblood of a freelance professional or business owner—but many of us feel an internal resistance to marketing. Why? Here are three reasons. Are there more than three? Sure! But the vast majority resist marketing for one of these:

- Our skill set focuses on a whole different direction (perhaps, creating products or delivering a service).
- We have a distaste for marketing and selling in general.
- We anticipate pain.

Here is a preview of some ideas explored in this book:

1. Our skill set focuses on a whole different direction (perhaps, creating products or delivering a service).

One of my friends is a software engineer. A brilliant one. He can write a program, and 98% of the time it runs perfectly the first time. No bugs. Over the years, I have talked with him about applying his brilliance to creating his own product and marketing it. Nothing ever happens, though. Why? He is simply not interested. He prefers to keep his head down and write software. There's nothing wrong with that. In fact, it appears best that he work for someone else and concentrate on his own interest and skill set.

On the other hand, since you're reading this book, odds are you're not that type. I trust you're looking to market your product, business, or service. How do you deal with marketing if it truly lies outside your skills and aptitudes? You can *hire contractors* for small parts of the marketing process. For example, to save my own time, I'll write a quick first draft of a description of one of my books. *Then I hire another writer* to revise the paragraph. Then I revise the paragraph again and place it online. This speeds up the process. (It works; I have 25 books on Amazon.com.)

This may seem like a minor example, but I invite you to pause for a moment. Some of us take pride in being able to "do things all by myself." That's okay. But when it breaks your momentum, you are the one who *gets really hurt.* (If you have a family, they lose out, too. Vacations never taken. A frustrating lifestyle.) Let's face it—if we're not good at something, we simply don't do it. That's where procrastination on marketing comes in.

The good news is: that 'something' that you're weak in is someone else's strong suit. Do *not* hesitate. Learn to delegate. *And it costs less than you think.* I was recently on a radio program, and I assured the host that one could hire, as one's editor, a part-time college English instructor for *a modest fee*. This book provides important techniques in how to delegate, listen, and lead a team of contractors.

2. We have a distaste for marketing and selling in general.

The classic phrase goes: "People like to buy but hate to be sold." Many of us feel pushed by overbearing salespeople—people who reek of desperation or manipulation. As a result, we dislike marketing and selling because we don't like those salespeople. We do not want to resemble them in any shape or fashion. The good news is: you do NOT need to be pushy like them, obnoxious like them, dishonest like them. It's better in fact to tell a story, one that entrances the buyer. This book helps you develop that story, your business image, and your position in the marketplace so that *people feel attracted* to you and your product or service.

3. We anticipate pain.

When marketing works, everyone feels joy. Customers get the right products, and you earn profits. However, when marketing goes wrong, you get nothing. No. Worse than nothing. You lose money. You lose customers. You lose dignity as you look at the failure of all the effort you put into that marketing campaign. The good news is: marketing pain is avoidable.

How do you avoid the pain of marketing? By using strategy, tactics and precision. This book provides strategies and tactics both. You'll find examples of how to position yourself and your business, how to identify your target market, and much more. Avoid going down any blind alleys. Save yourself the pain!

9-Minute Method (#1): Connect with *Want Power*

Why You Need to Do This:

Successful people I have interviewed demonstrate one characteristic in particular: They want something. A lot! Even in myself, I've noticed that *Want Power* can overcome anticipation of both pain and inconvenience. So the reason to connect with your Want Power is to give yourself the best chances for success.

To overcome the three difficulties that I mentioned above, you need an "irresistible force"—Want Power. How is Want Power irresistible? Imagine you've just finished dinner and you dread washing dishes. Then your spouse (or roommate) says, "After you finish the dishes and I take out the garbage, let's see that movie you really want to see!" Suddenly, your desire to view the film energizes you to complete the dishes in record time. You found energy you did not know you had. That's the benefit of Want Power.

Every great accomplishment began with someone wanting to see it come to reality. Steve Jobs said that he wanted his team to "make a dent in the universe." Steve focused on innovation and product design. Each time he would unveil a new product, people would wait with baited breath. "An iPod, a phone, an internet mobile communicator... these are NOT three separate devices! And we are calling it iPhone! Today Apple is going to reinvent the phone. And here it is," Steve said at MacWorld 2007. Steve summarized what he wanted: "Being the richest man in the cemetery doesn't matter to me. Going to bed at night saying we've done something wonderful, that's what matters to me."

Disneyland exists because Walt Disney *wanted* to see something manifested. Walt said, "Disneyland really began when my two daughters were very young. Saturday was always 'Daddy's Day' and I would take them to the merry-go-round and sit on a bench eating peanuts, while they rode. And sitting there alone, I felt that something should be built, some kind of family park where parents and children could have fun together." So what did Walt do? He pulled together a team and created something the world had never seen before—a theme park. Disneyland and Walt Disney World remain in the top five of theme parks the world over.

The Exercise:

In nine minutes, answer these questions:

- Why did you start your business?
- What is the fun part of what you do?
- What do you feel good about—related to how you help people?
- Which part of your business would you do exclusively—if you could?

- What do you long to see accomplished? What is your vision?
- How would you reward yourself (or your family) when you achieve those big profits?

These answers alert you to experiences and items that you want. Take these answers and post them where you can see them. Use these answers as the basis of your Want Power. Review them daily. Stay focused and energize yourself to create your marketing campaign. Start with your end goal in mind. You'll get more done, and you'll feel proud of yourself.

* * *

So we began with Want Power. An old phrase is: "A person with a big enough Why can endure any How." In other words, when you *want* something a lot, you'll put in the effort to learn and practice effective methods. At this point I also want to share with you a method to make marketing an easy process.

Marketing Made Easy

How can you experience marketing as an easy process? It's all about making an easy system. Here's an example. Someone calls a speaker-author, Mai. She doesn't have to think about her process; she just opens her Marketing Plan (in a binder) and goes through these steps:

1. Receive inquiry from a new prospective client.
2. Answer questions during the call and inquire about what the person needs and wants.
3. During the call, offer a choice of three free articles.
4. Email the chosen article to the prospective client.
5. Make a follow-up call and …

You see that Mai doesn't have to start from scratch with each incoming phone call. She has a plan.

And this is how you can make your marketing easy. As you read this book, jot down ideas that impress you as: "That sounds good. I can try that." Place your notes on methods and the ten marketing strengths in a binder, using tabs to organize the elements. Soon you will have your own marketing plan. I call this the "Easy Part Start."

* * *

Here's something else that will bring ease to your life. Hire a few contractors. As I mentioned this quote earlier: "Nothing is impossible for [the person] who doesn't have to do it himself [herself]." Along the lines of working with contractors, Linda Finkle will guide us in leading a virtual workforce:

The Communication Skills Needed in Managing a Virtual Workforce

by Linda Finkle

A lot of our activities go around the digital world these days, and many businesses are figuring out that they can opt to not have their employees work onsite. Individuals can now work anywhere they are able to access the internet, making outsourcing and being employed by someone halfway across the globe possible. It's a true test of communication skills to be able to manage a virtual workforce, whether working with an individual or a whole team, so how do we go about this?

Most entrepreneurs working with a virtual workforce

often find themselves struggling with issues of communication, work control, productivity and accountability. If you wish to make your workforce and your management over your workforce more efficient, good communication skills are a must. I say this because a lot of non-verbal aspects of communication, like hand gestures, body language and tonality, which add to how well you communicate with people, are not involved when it comes to managing people virtually.

That being said, here are some points to ponder if you wish to be efficient in working with a virtual workforce:

1. Be clear in the definition of objectives and what you expect of them.

If your virtual workforce is unclear about your organizational objectives or do not know exactly what it is they need to perform, too much time will be spent in having to go back and forth with questions and answers instead of actually getting some work done.

This is when an excellent grasp of written communication skills comes into play, where you need to be able to explain the requirements of the job in a clear and concise manner.

2. Keep everyone on the same page.

Whether it's just the two of you working together or you managing an entire off-site team, keep communication lines open where you can all converse and collaborate. With office employees, you have a greater level of interaction and monitoring but with virtual employees, you need to employ other avenues, like mailing groups or file sharing sites, for which they can share and collaborate on ideas.

3. Make them feel connected.

Working with employees virtually doesn't mean that your off-site staff is any less important that your office employees. Ensure that they are equally connected with your organization by keeping them informed about all major decisions and reminding them of the importance of their roles in achieving your organization's objectives.

4. Find a single partner for multiple virtual services.

You may have virtual employees for non-core business tasks, or you may have picked only a handful of activities for them to do. It helps if you find a single partner who could provide you with a combination of professional and managed services so that you can collaborate easily and get things done the way you want through a single source instead of managing multiple providers, saving you hours of hassle and extra costs.

All things considered, it's really in your *communication skills* and how you communicate what you want accomplished and how you want it done that determines how efficient your virtual workforce will be.

About Linda Finkle:

Communication is the number one challenge in organizations. Linda Finkle of Incedo Group has for over twelve years worked with businesses and partnerships helping to bring about changes in the way people communicate. Of course, company profitability is an inevitable side effect, but at least as important is partners and employees have more fun.

Linda combines insight, humor, and tons of good, old-fashioned common sense to create, not just a dialogue, but a total experience which yields instant and ongoing results. Linda is a Master Certified Coach and holds a bachelor's degree from Ohio University. Her recent book Finding the Fork in the Road reached best seller status on Amazon.com.

Reach Linda at Incedo Group, LLC
linda@incedogroup.com 301.315.2420 www.incedogroup.com

* * *

Above Linda Finkle shared details of leading a virtual team. To lead such a team, it helps to have a clear vision. You'll lead with confidence when you have such a vision (embodied in a mission statement). Next, you'll learn to convert Want Power into a mission statement; Dr. Tony Alessandra shows the way.

Hidden Power for Your Marketing

by Dr. Tony Alessandra

You need a clearly defined mission to be successful! To get anything significant accomplished, you must work hard, possess energy, and demonstrate drive. But to truly influence others, you also need a mission.

It isn't enough just to come up with a "mission statement" that merely sounds good or looks sharp on paper, though that's a start. Instead, to be effective, your mission has got to come from your heart. It's got to grow out of a sense of what's important in your life and in your world.

The most effective missions involve helping others. Often, it's acquiring that mission that catapults people into a leadership role, which puts them in a position to exercise personal power.

Steve Jobs and Steve Wozniak didn't start up Apple Computer just to make money or to make people more efficient; their mission was to develop a "user-friendly" machine that would revolutionize people's lives. Their sense of purpose propelled them to perform brilliantly. And, characteristically, when they later sought to attract John Sculley, widely respected as a marvelous marketer, they didn't emphasize money or prestige, both of which he already had in abundance as Pepsi's president and CEO.

Instead, according to Sculley's autobiography, Jobs and Sculley were walking near Sculley's home when Jobs asked, "So, what do you want to do, John? Do you want to sell sugared water for the rest of your life—or do you want a chance to change the world?" Sculley, faced with that kind of challenge and that kind of vision, knew what he had to do. He acquired a new mission and joined Apple.

Candy Lightner's defining moment came in 1980 when her daughter Cari was killed by a drunk driver. Her anger soon turned into her mission: a burning desire to do something about such wasteful tragedies. Within a few days, she held a meeting with a few friends—and that was the beginning of Mothers Against Drunk Driving, better known as MADD. Candy Lightner had no position of power when she began. Yet she is living proof of Andrew Jackson's famous epigram: "One man with courage makes a majority." Or, in this case, one woman. "If you care enough," Lightner says, "you can accomplish anything."

As usual, your attitude can affect how you choose to frame your mission. Perhaps you look around and say, "Here I am, stuck in a dead-end job. How can I possibly develop a mission?"

But where we are, or what happens to us, is not as important as what we think about where we are or what happens to us. My point is, maybe we can't all have missions echoing the grand but simple nobility espoused by Salvation Army founder William Booth: "Others." But we can all look outside ourselves as we try to figure out our life's purpose. And looking outside ourselves will not only help us fashion a mission, it will also help draw people to us and our mission.

Spell out your own success with SMART goal-setting: Striving for and attaining goals makes life meaningful. Goals create drive—but only if you set yourself to achieving them in the proper way. I have found that the letters in the word SMART are very useful in articulating goals.

SMART reminds me that my goals must be Specific, Measurable, Action-Oriented, Realistic & Relevant, and Time-Bound.

Specific and Measurable relate to how you phrase your goal. Vagueness goes hand in hand with lack of genuine commitment. You do not think a world-class pole-vaulter, for instance, just says, "I want to jump higher next year." No, he has a certain height in mind.

Therefore, instead of "I will be more fit in six months so I can hike into mountains and help with a reforestation project," you might say, "In six months my resting blood pressure will be ten points lower."

Alternatively, "In six months I'll be twenty pounds lighter." "I'll be running three miles in four to six months" is more effective than "I'll be running more in four to six months."

Or if your goal is to become a standout salesperson so you eventually can rise in the firm and change its focus, you'd be better off proclaiming, "I will increase my sales next year by twenty percent" rather than "I will sell more next year."

In order to ensure your goal is Measurable, you need to know if you are making progress. You need to set up interim goals or checkpoints along the way. Depending on what your goal is, you might be checking your progress every day, once a week, or once every two months.

Action-Oriented means that your goal will involve taking

action. We cannot move toward our goals by standing still, and stating your goals in such a way that denotes action releases the power that you inherently have available internally. The statements above include the action that will be taken. Words like "hike" and "running" make the goal real, powerful, and motivating.

Realistic has to do with the goal, which should be just beyond your reach, making you stretch. It should be attainable, yet challenging. The goal must also be Relevant to your overall plan and direction or it will be a distraction or have a detrimental impact on your overall goals and aspirations.

If it is almost impossible to achieve, a goal can be de-motivating. On the other hand, a goal with 100 percent chance of achievement is not really a goal; it is a given. That defeats the purpose of goals, which is to move you forward by making you work harder, or by gathering more resources than you had in the past.

The last rule of smart goal setting is Time-Bound. Until you set a specific time frame in which your goal will be accomplished, it is merely a wish, not a goal. Set the exact time that the goal will be accomplished, and if it is a longer-term goal (over three months), you

should also set up short-term checkpoints when you will measure progress, and take corrective action in order to get back on track if necessary.

You may discover that your goal is not attainable or realistic within the time frame you have set. However, be flexible about your game plan before you reconsider your goal. Nothing ever goes exactly according to plan, so you may have to make adjustments in order to stay on track and keep up your motivation.

Some other suggestions about goals:

—Write them down. It's one thing to think about your goals, but it's quite another to dignify them by putting them on paper. Trust me on this! Writing them down makes them more tangible, more meaningful, and more imperative. Instead of being nothing more than a vague musing, your list of goals becomes a call to arms, a goad to action, and a pact with yourself.

—Make them personal. They must be sincere and something you want to do rather than something you think you should do. Whatever your objective, the reasons must be strong enough to fuel your desire to work to attain your goal.

—Make them positive. The mind cannot refuse to think of something when instructed to do so. So if you say, "I will not smoke today," your mind automatically ends up thinking more about smoking than if you had said, "I will breathe only clean air today." Same purpose—more effective.

Recognized by Meetings & Conventions Magazine as "one of America's most electrifying speakers," **Dr. Tony Alessandra** was inducted into the Speakers Hall of Fame in 1985. In 2009, he was inducted as one of the "Legends of the Speaking Profession;" in 2010, 2011 & 2012, he was selected as one of the Top 5 Marketing Speakers by Speaking.com; in 2010, Tony was elected into the inaugural class of the Sales Hall of Fame; in 2012, he was voted one of the Top 50 Sales & Marketing Influencers; and also in 2012, Dr. Tony was voted the #1 World's Top Communication Guru. Tony's polished style, powerful message, and proven ability as a consummate business strategist consistently earn rave reviews and loyal clients.

In addition to being president of

AssessmentBusinessCenter.com, a company that offers online 360º assessments, Tony is also a founding partner in the

PlatinumRule.com—a company which has successfully combined cutting-edge technology and proven psychology to give salespeople the ability to build and maintain positive relationships with hundreds of clients and prospects.

Dr. Alessandra is a prolific author with 27 books translated into over 50 foreign language editions, including the newly revised, best-selling *The New Art of Managing People*. He is featured in over 100 audio/video programs and films, including *Relationship Strategies.*

Products: http://www.alessandra.com/products/index.asp

* * *

Above, Dr. Tony Alessandra encouraged us to develop our mission statement and SMART goals. Along these lines, a big message of this book is: Get started now! It really helps to get to the heart of the matter . . .

What Are You Really Marketing?

If you were selling soap, what are you really marketing? Feeling clean.

I recall TV commercials in which beaming people enjoyed feeling "Zestfully clean" (Zest is a brand of soap).

I was working with an intern and the question arose: "What are we really marketing?" With three of my books, we notice:

- *Be Heard and Be Trusted*—"a relationship that brings good feelings or what you want [trust will get you a closed sale]"
- *Truth No One Will Tell You*—"hope"
- *Nothing Can Stop You This Year*—"comfort and encouragement"

So now with your product or service ... what are you really marketing?

* * *

If you're a self-employed professional, you are also marketing yourself as part of the product or service you're offering. Now C.J. Hayden guides us in crucial marketing strategies.

If You Want to Get Clients, You'll Have to Talk to Them
by C.J. Hayden, MCC

"I've done everything I can think of to get clients," a desperate self-employed professional wrote to me. "I launched a website, I had a brochure designed, I've been sending out mailings, and I've placed all sorts of ads in print and on the web. But no one is hiring me. What am I doing wrong?"

This unhappy professional has made a common mistake. She has fallen into the trap of believing that spending money on marketing materials, mailings, and ads will somehow produce clients without the direct involvement of the business owner. And she truly believes that this is "everything" she can do.

Perhaps professionals who make this mistake are trying to follow the model of big business.

They hide behind a company name, expensive marketing literature, and a website. They spend hundreds or thousands of dollars on ads, directory listings, and trade show booths. Far too many self-employed professionals don't even disclose their own name in their marketing, even when they are operating a one-person company!

But people don't buy professional services from an anonymous company whose name they don't even recognize; they buy them from either: 1) nationally recognized firms who have spent millions to gain name recognition, or 2) individual people they have learned to know, like, and trust. The more personal — or the more expensive — the service you offer is, the more likely this is to be true.

If you are a financial advisor, career counselor, or life coach, you are asking people to trust you with the most intimate areas of their lives. If you are a web designer, IT consultant, or corporate trainer, you are asking your clients to trust you enough to spend thousands of dollars with you. You don't earn people's trust by placing an ad or sending them a brochure.

Independent professionals and small professional services firms simply don't have the resources to build name recognition and trust by way of high-priced, anonymous approaches like advertising and mass mailings. In fact, the approaches that work best for most professionals to get clients are less expensive—and more personal.

Here are the five best ways for professionals to get clients:

1. Meeting prospects or referral sources in person, at events or by appointment
2. Talking to prospects or referral sources on the phone
3. Sending personal letters and emails to prospects who already know them
4. Following up personally with prospects over time
5. Speaking to groups likely to contain prospects at meetings and conferences

And here are the five things self-employed professionals most often try that don't result in clients:

1. Placing ads in the Yellow Pages, trade publications, or pay-per-click ads on the web
2. Distributing or posting brochures or flyers around

their community

3. Mailing mass-produced letters or brochures to strangers
4. Sending their newsletter or ezine to people who haven't asked for it
5. Building a website consisting of nothing but promotional copy for people to read

The main difference between these two lists is that the first group of approaches require you to talk to people. The second list consists of anonymous activities that allow you to hide out and never meet the people you are in business to serve.

If you want people to become your clients, they need to get to know you, learn to like you, and believe they can trust you. And for that, they really do need to meet you.

It is understandable why so many business owners gravitate to the least effective marketing tactics — they are so much easier to accomplish! To buy an ad, all you have to do is put up the money. To send a mailing, all you need is a mailing list and postage. It's much more challenging to go out and meet strangers, or to call people on the phone, or to speak in public.

But the reality is that this is what it takes to get clients. Even if you have the world's most

compelling copy on your website, it's a rare client who finds their way to your site, reads it, and decides then and there to work with you. The same is true for an ad or a brochure. All these marketing tools are simply that—tools. Just like a pair of pliers, they need a person holding them in order for them to work.

What clients want is to get a sense of who you are as a person. They want to see your face or hear your voice, to get to know you over time. If you don't have enough confidence in your business to speak to people in person about it, how will they ever have enough confidence in you to hire you?

What you'll discover if you begin to meet prospects in person, talk to them on the phone, and speak with them directly about how you can help them, is that it gets easier the more you do it. It will build your confidence in yourself—and the confidence your prospective clients have in you—at the same time.

If you're in the business of serving people, your best marketing tool can be your own voice. So put it to work and start talking to them.

C.J. Hayden is the author of *Get Clients Now!*™ Thousands of business owners and independent professionals have used her simple sales and marketing system to double or triple their income. Get a free copy of "Five Secrets to Finding All the Clients You'll Ever Need" at www.getclientsnow.com.

* * *

Now that you have found some ideas about what you're really marketing, let's take the next step. Develop some clarity in your marketing message:

How Does the Marketer Gain Clarity?

How do you boil down your marketing message to a simple, clear, impactful statement? A mile of ink, a hill of printed pages and twenty earfuls of talk. That is, you try a lot of things; you talk with a number of people … and you explore.

For example, one of my interns was working on a revision of one of my websites. He proposed the catchphrase: "Leverage yourself above everyone." Did that fit as a description of what I do? Well, it was a bold statement.

But I hesitated. It did not feel like me. On one hand, I certainly like "leverage" and I have spoken on "Time Leverage" for years. But the "above everyone" had my colleagues and me hesitating. For instance, I'm the "Be Heard and Be Trusted" guy. (*Be Heard and Be Trusted* is the title of one of my books.) I am not into ruthless competition.

Here's the solution (for now): we use "leverage your best life." In marketing, I like the words "you" and "your" for getting attention.

Am I done with "leverage your best life"? Probably not. But this catchphrase is currently on the website and doing its job—until a better idea comes along.

* * *

As I mentioned earlier, many of us resist marketing. Fear comprises a big component. What if there was a way to reduce or quiet down that fear? Often, you can reduce fear if you have some crucial information. Brian Tracy's below Four Key Questions help a great deal.

Four Key Questions to Consider When Developing Your Marketing Plan for Products and Services

by Brian Tracy

When creating your marketing plan, there are four key questions that you must consider as frequently as possible, to test any ideas you may have for products and services.

Key Question 1: Is there really a market?

The first of the four key questions you must consider for your marketing plan is if there are people who will actually buy your products and services. There may be a good reason why other companies aren't making these products and services available. To discover the answer, great companies try several variations of the product side by side and see which works best for customers.

The only real test is a market test. Only live customers can tell you if you have a winner or not. Get a prototype, a model, or a written description or picture, and test the new products and services in the marketplace. Offer it, sell it, or give it away to customers and see how they respond.

Whatever you do, aim for immediate feedback. Don't be shy. Get responses from those you will expect to buy the products and services as soon as they are available. In most cases, your initial product or service idea is deficient in some way. But by changing it in response to customer comments or complaints, you may develop products and services that become a market leader.

When developing your marketing plan, always assume that a competitor is rushing to bring similar products and services to the market. Develop a bias for action. Avoid paralysis by analysis. Instill a sense of urgency at all times.

Key Question 2: Is the market big enough to make it worthwhile pursuing?

Another one of the key questions to consider for your marketing plan is if the market is large enough to justify all the time, trouble, effort, and expense necessary to develop the products and services and bring them to market? Can you sell enough of your products and services to make it economically worthwhile? There are many products and services for which there is a definite market, but the market is too small to make it worth pursuing. Market research in this area can be invaluable in helping you to make the right decision when developing your marketing plan.

Key Question 3: Is the market for your products and services concentrated enough?

Assuming that there is demand for your product, and the demand is large enough, do the means of advertising and promoting the product exist that would enable you to sell to that market in a cost-effective way?

In his book *The Long Tail: Why the Future of Business Is Selling Less of More,* Chris Anderson argues that when the major competitors fight over selling the most popular books and movies, the profit margins for those few "big hits" get slammed. Blockbuster movies and books tend to get deeply discounted in price by big retailers and flame out in popularity quickly. In contrast, specialized products have a "long tail"—they stay popular in smaller quantities and are sold at higher margins by more specialized retailers. Instead of going after the obvious blockbusters, Anderson advises savvy marketers can go after narrower, more specialized segments of customer groups all over the world.

Online services make accessibility to these unique customers easier and cheaper than ever. At the same time, however, the lower costs of entry also mean that more retailers are competing for the attention of consumers in every aspect of electronic commerce and making it harder to cash in on the long tail.

Key Question 4: Who is your competition?

Lastly, one of the key questions you must consider for your marketing plan is who are your main competitors in the market? Even if your product isn't out there (yet), there will always be competition for the customer's dollar. That's how you should think about it when developing your marketing plan. Remember, the overwhelming majority of new product or service offerings fail because there is no market, or the market is not large enough, or the market is not concentrated enough to be reached in a cost-effective manner, or your competitor's offerings are superior to yours in some way.

Thank you for reading this article on the four key questions to consider when developing your marketing plan for your products and services.

Brian Tracy is the most listened to audio author on personal and business success in the world today. His fast-moving talks and seminars on leadership, sales, managerial effectiveness and business strategy are loaded with powerful, proven ideas and strategies that people can immediately apply to get better results in every area. For more information, please go to www.briantracy.com

* * *

In conclusion, we've discussed how many of us resist marketing. Then we went through the process of developing our Want Power. Using a mission statement and creating SMART goals—plus gaining clarity about our marketing message—all help us stamp out procrastination and begin forming our marketing campaign.

Here are details my clients have thought through for a marketing campaign:

- I'll send a marketing message to 5,000 esubscribers (on a colleague's elist) and anticipate a 1% response.
- I'll send a direct marketing piece of mail to a targeted list of 300 people. I'll send a first message that includes a coupon to all 300. Then for the people who do not call in to activate their coupon,

I'll send a second mailing. Finally, for the people who still have not responded, I'll send a third message. (Marketing expert Dan Kennedy reports that a process like this can yield up to a 17% response rate.)

Points to Remember:

*** Secret #1: Many of us resist marketing.**

*** Your Countermeasure:**
Develop your Want Power. Identify your mission statement and form your SMART goals. Get started today.

* * * * * *

Secret #2: People procrastinate because they don't connect money spent on marketing with immediate results.

Have you tried some form of marketing, and you did not see an immediate result? If so, I empathize. Let me encourage you: Every forward step you take plants seeds for success to blossom. How? To get more opportunities, you need to be "in front of" more people. And sometimes the numbers do not feel encouraging. Some forms of marketing like direct mail yield on average 1% in sales. And some marketers think that's pretty good considering the medium.

In any case, when you invest in marketing, you often invest for the long term.

9-Minute Method (#2): Use Effort-Goals and Result-Goals

Why You Need to Do This:

As I implied above, by its very nature, marketing plants

seeds today for a later harvest. Here's a quick example. Let's say you start making cold phone calls. Many professionals call it a "numbers game." Why? Because often a person must go through thirty "no's" before getting one "Yes, I'll buy your product." The reason you use both Effort-Goals and Result-Goals is to keep up your spirits and your personal energy so that you make those 31 calls!

In the beginning, you will need to make many calls to find even one new one client. Frustrating, but unavoidably true. Let's call "one new client" your Result-Goal. That's the result you want. How many calls will it take to gain that new client? For that, you can use an Effort-Goal—which relates to your personal efforts, something under your direct control.

Consider starting with an Effort-Goal of making 10 calls per day for three days every week.

Here is an important distinction: Your Result-Goal often depends on external elements (for example: the mood of the prospective client). On the other hand, your Effort-Goal resides directing under your control. You are in charge of making each phone call.

What is the point of all this? Why set a Result-Goal and a separate Effort-Goal? It's about human nature. If you don't keep score, you won't feel you're making any progress. And that feels bad. Many of us will simply stop doing any activity that feels bad.

However, now you have a strategy to keep up your own morale and personal energy. By using the Result-Goal/Effort-Goal process, you transform the bad feelings related to "no connection of marketing to immediate results." Consider repeating this affirmation to yourself: "I plant marketing seeds today so that I can harvest more profits tomorrow."

The Exercise:

Take the next nine minutes and write down two possible Effort-Goals and two possible Result-Goals for your own marketing.

* * *

We covered the Result-Goal/Effort-Goal process so that you can start to realize the seed planting-later-harvest reality of marketing. Now, we'll explore another empowering way to set goals. Goal-setting is essential for both marketing and for maintaining personal energy and focus to accomplish such marketing.

How You Can Set a Marketing Campaign Goal to Expand Your Mind and Your Profits

Have you ever set a marketing goal and felt overwhelmed? Some of us set goals that are too small; and others set goals that are too tough. Either way, you might drain your energy.

Now, learn an empowering way to set goals that can get you to think in new ways and to achieve extraordinary results. This process was innovated by author Raymond Aaron, and he calls it "MTO" (Minimum, Target and Outrageous).

Here's an example—my client Kerrie sets these goals:

Monthly Goals:

- Minimum: Sell 11 books on Amazon.com—per month
- Target: Sell 33 books
- Outrageous: Sell 3,000 books

If she sells 11 books, she is still happy. The magic happens when she considers how to sell 3,000 books. Her mind starts flowing with new possibilities to try. To sell 3,000 books she might want to contact other authors who have e-subscriber lists. To sell 2% (3,000 copies) she would need to make an arrangement with 8 authors, each with a list of approximately 20,000 e-subscribers.

You can see how this goal-setting process is empowering. Now try the "MTO" process on one of your first-guess goals.

* * *

The situation of "procrastinating because you don't connect the money you spend on marketing today with immediate results" calls for a *transformation*—a change from one mindset to another. Now Willie Jolley will demonstrate a mindset that will power you up to get more done.

Make Something Happen!
by Willie Jolley

What's more important than a business plan? I believe you need a hustle plan.

For example, when I was just starting my speaking business, I took audacious action. I knew that members of the National Association of College Activities Convention were choosing speakers for the year. But I didn't have money to pay the registration fee so I couldn't enter the convention hall. I didn't let that stop me. I gave out my little flyers about my speaking business outside the convention hall.

Soon, my friend twice admonished me to stop handing out flyers: "Man, this is not how we do it. You are embarrassing yourself!" After he left that second time, I started back up and continued until I had given out all of my flyers.

Later, a man hollered at me when I walked past the convention hall. I thought he was security and was going to yell at me about breaking rules. Instead, he asked if I had been the guy giving out the flyers in the morning.

"Yes. I confess … it was me!"

"Good!" he replied, "I have been looking for you all day! I am the owner of the biggest college booking agency, and I think that if you have enough guts to hustle and work like you did today, then I think you will be a help to our agency."

From this moment when my hustling paid off, he became my biggest booking agent for colleges!

When asked what keeps them from being successful, most people will blame the government, the economy, their families, or the "isms" of life (you know … sexism, racism, ageism, etc.). But the one thing most people avoid in their list is that which is most important! It is the person we see every day in the mirror … it is us! We are the main obstacles to our success in life! Instead, we must make things happen.

It has been stated, and I believe it is true, that success follows the 80/20 rule: 80 percent of the work usually comes from 20 percent of the people. In personal achievement, this means we are responsible for 80 percent of our failure to hit our goals, and outside obstacles are only 20 percent of the problem.

The old African proverb states, "If you can overcome the enemy on the inside, the enemy on the outside can do you no harm!" We must be brutally honest with ourselves and come to the realization that we are the biggest challenge to our own success!

If you want to win, you must stop letting things happen and start making things happen. Remember, when all is said and done, much more is said than done … so let's go get it done!

Today … make a commitment to overcome yourself, so

you can reach your goals!

During tough economic times, some people sit and wait for the economy to change. They talk about how bad things are, and they just want to survive the storms. Yet there are others who do not wait for things to happen, they make things happen.

This article includes Willie's story of handing out flyers that is one highlight from his book *Turn Setbacks into Greenbacks*.

Willie Jolley is America's premier celebrity speaker-singer-author ... inspiring millions with music and motivation! Success Magazine hailed Willie Jolley as the "Comeback King"—when he successfully helped Ford Motors avert the need to accept bail out dollars. Ford took Willie on a speaking tour to present to all their employees. Willie was named "One of the Outstanding Five Speakers in the World" by Toastmasters International. Willie earned the CPAE/Speaker Hall of Fame Award from the National Speakers Association. Willie authored the best-selling book *A Setback Is A Setup For A Comeback.* Willie's wealth-building book *Turn Setbacks Into Greenbacks* is on its way to becoming another bestseller. Willie hosts "The Willie Jolley Weekend Show" on XM Satellite radio. He holds a B.A. in Psychology and Sociology from The American University and a Masters Degree from Wesley Theological Seminary. His mission in life is to help people maximize their God-given talents and abilities so they can "Do More, Be More and Achieve More!"

Visit WillieJolley.com 202-723-8863 info@williejolley.com

* * *

Like any good coach, Willie encourages us to take action. Many of us fail to take action because fear paralyzes us and we lack a potent overall vision that can power-through such fear.

A Word About Fear

Many of the best things that have happened in my life occurred when I faced into the wind of fear and took action.

Do the thing we fear, and death of fear is certain.

– Ralph Waldo Emerson

If you take small steps, perhaps, do a mailing to only 300 people, you can quiet down some of your fear. Fear may even be absent from some moments. But it comes back. When you're stretching and learning, you come up against situations in which you fear adverse outcomes. And so I've learned to live with fear. In fact, I coined a phrase: "Fear keeps you on the mountain." By that, I mean that fear reminds you to take efforts to prepare and fear keeps you alert.

Preparation and staying alert are useful for creating a marketing plan.

Test It By Product

Here's a method to reduce fear by reducing the amount of money at risk. For example, if I consider writing a book and then publishing it as a paperback, I go through a process:

1) I write a blog article and observe how many people share the article on Facebook.

2) If the article is shared more than 20 times, I start to feel that there may be suitable interest.

3) I'll write a short ebook and see how it does on Amazon.com and BarnesandNoble.com. (Placement of the ebook on those websites is free!)

I incur only modest costs for editing and the cover design for an ebook.

You'll never know if your product will arrive in the marketplace at the right time. I suggest that you find ways to *test the product-concept for little or no cost* (like my above ebook example).

In this way, you reduce the risk and the related fear. You take action. Good!

Points to Remember:

*** Secret #2: People procrastinate because they don't connect money spent on marketing with immediate results.**

*** Your Countermeasure:**

Transform your impression about marketing. Start with setting a Result-Goal and related Effort-Goals. Take action. See how your initial efforts pan out. If necessary, modify your efforts and try something new. Marketing requires experimenting and evaluating such experiments.

* * * * * *

Secret #3: People procrastinate because they're afraid of losing money.

It's understandable that you're afraid of losing money. So do something that only costs your time and thinking. Define your business image. If you come up with a good business image, you won't waste money going down the "wrong alley." When you feel clear on your business image, you quiet down some of the fear of losing money.

9-Minute Method (#3): Pick 5 Power Words

Why You Need to Do This:

What is your business image? How can people pick your business to provide a product or service if they do not know you? They need to know you so well that they can describe to themselves or others what you do in five words or less. An example I mentioned earlier is how Disney embodies two words: "family entertainment." Then there's Kleenex—"facial tissue."

In essence, coming up with your "five power words" is the heart of your business image. It can also be the center of your marketing campaign for a particular product or service. And that's the reason we need you to focus on five such words.

We need you to access your intuition. Why? Two reasons: a) marketers can get stuck in trying to rationally analyze the essence of a product's appeal and b) customers make buying decisions based on their feelings so we want to access our own feelings. Here's the problem with starting with a merely rational analysis: When I was in grade school, I was pushed to write a formal outline with a hierarchy of topics and subtopics. Trying to do that process rationally made for slow going. But I could do better by first brainstorming ideas onto a page and then sorting them. So consider the following exercise as your chance to do some brainstorming and accessing your intuition.

The Exercise:

In the next nine minutes, answer the following questions quickly. Just give your first impressions. Don't hesitate. Just write quickly:

1) What does your product/service do for your client?

Examples: provides fun, relieves stress

2) How does your client experience a transformation*?

(That is, how does the client become stronger, happier, or some other beneficial state of being?)

Examples: Stronger, happier, more skillful, confident, persuasive

3) What makes you/your business different?

Examples: get to the heart of the matter, discover opportunities, provide solutions

* * *

**** A Word About Transformation***

What is your customer really buying? A transformation. Somehow in their current life there is a gap between what they want and what their current reality is. Focus on the transformation (big improvement) that they want. Many marketers get the process mixed up. They emphasize something like "Get 9 CDs in this program." The potential customer thinks: "9 CDs. That's 9 hours. I don't have that kind of time." Instead, focus on how the person will gain tangible confidence with which they can improve their sales by 37%. Entice the person by getting them to think about how *they will transform into someone who confidently and easily persuades and motivates buyers.* People are not buying the delivery mode (like CDs or 7 hours of downloaded material). They are buying the transformation. What they're really buying is the *anticipated good feelings* they expect to feel.

* * *

Now, what do you do with the answers to the above questions? Identify five words that embody for you (at this moment) the essence of your product or service. Above we talked about defining your business image. You have actually begun the process of "creating a brand." But I did not use that phrase because many readers would emotionally shut down, having thoughts like: "That's my problem. Creating a brand sounds too complicated and too hard for me. What if I make a mistake?!"

I want to encourage you to take some steps forward. Sometimes, in the moment, a step may seem like a mistake but it is really a rung on a ladder to success. For example, I released a book under the title *Communicate to Win,* and I hoped that I had the right title and the right marketing campaign. That title did fine. Not great. But fine. However, I saw an *increase* in sales when I re-released the book as a new edition under the title of *Be Heard and Be Trusted.*

Do I regret releasing the book under the first title? Not at all. Why? Because I was making progress all along. In fact, *Communicate to Win* led to the first time I taught the college course Technical Communication. Also, under the title *Communicate to Win,* the book joined other items in the Cogswell Polytechnical College Time Capsule to be opened in 2100. The Time Capsule detail helped build my personal brand.

I have no regrets about the releasing/re-titling situation because a) I made money as I went along, b) I gained new work and new customers, and c) I got to the essence of what I do as part of my lifework.

This section is about handling the fear of losing money. With my example about the book that became *Be Heard and Be Trusted* (and which birthed my blog

BeHeardandBeTrusted.com), I demonstrate that I built my brand. You do *not* lose money if you build your brand. Instead, you are investing your money for the long-term health of your business.

An important element of building your brand is the *power of simplicity.* If you cannot bring your product down to just five words, then you do not really know your product. For example, this book is the eighth entry in my *Darkest Secrets . . . How to Protect Yourself* series. I can identify what these books bring to the reading public: Strength and Self-protection. There you have it: three words. These words resonate with my own feelings. Now, one of my editors said, "Your books provide exercises to develop focus, understanding and courage which then become personal strength." I include this example to demonstrate that marketing is truly a journey and a process. Often, it does not take place with one book title, one marketing campaign, or one slogan. You need to step into the marketplace and allow clients and customers to "tell you" what you do that *works for them.*

Counter the Fear of Losing Money: Start with Social Media

When you hesitate to launch a marketing campaign, see if you can test some details through social media. Start marketing and testing for free! How? I try things out with my blog. As I mentioned earlier, I'll write a blog article and see how many people share the article on Facebook. If an article is shared 10 times, that gives me a bit of information. If another article is shared 45 times, then I start to consider that I have struck a resonant chord with some readers. I also note how often the article is shared on LinkedIn.com.

Further, I notice the situation when I do a particular topic for a blogtalk.com online radio interview. For example, when 41 people clicked "like" for my topic "How to Be Emotionally Strong and Make Your Dreams Come True," I started thinking, "Perhaps, I may do a new product built around this topic." *You see how this is a process of testing ideas without spending money!*

Here is an important principle: You do NOT lose money by building your brand.

Every time you enter the marketplace, you create an image in your potential customer's mind. Whether through social media or other forms of marketing, develop your marketing message. Make your brand something enticing in your customer's mind, and you take steps forward.

* * *

Let's continue our discussion about handling the fear of losing money. One tough truth to bear is that some of your marketing campaigns will yield small results. You never really know what will happen. You'll need to bring something to the marketplace to see what people will respond to. Getting small results is a worst-case scenario. You still need to do marketing campaigns so that you refine your marketing message and build your way to a subsequent hugely successful marketing campaign.

The good news is that you can increase your odds for success with a marketing campaign and you can reduce the downside. And this leads us to three practices I use for dealing with fear:

1. Reduce the downside.
2. Preset the safety net.
3. Use fear to jumpstart preparation.

1. Reduce the downside

Develop your plans so that you avoid making a big investment if possible. When I say, "reduce the downside," I mean reduce possible negative outcomes. One way is to use a modest budget. Another way is to identify a more potent strategy. For example, Susan has a local retail business. Instead of paying for 5,000 names for a one-time direct mailing campaign, she employs a more potent strategy: She gets a targeted list of 300 names. Her plan is to a do a three-step mailing.

Step 1: She sends a coupon/special offer to the 300 names

and addresses.

Step 2: She sends a second mailing to those people who still did not call in and activate the offer.

Step 3: She sends a third mailing to the remaining people who did not call in.

She paid less for a smaller list, and she paid less for sending out 600 pieces of mail instead of 5,000 pieces. However, she gets better results. Why? She gets a better response rate because some of the people *received two or three repeated exposures* to her message.

Another way to reduce the downside is to begin your marketing efforts by testing something and *not* spending money. Above, I shared with you my experience with testing ideas that may result in a later book or audio product. As I mentioned, I watch the responses to my articles—the number of shares on Facebook, Linkedin, and Twitter.

You can also reduce the downside by making a less costly test-version of a product. My next example relates to books and ebooks. Here's how I reduce the downside of having my company publish a new book. I write a short ebook *first*—perhaps, 117 pages. I only need to have a graphic artist create the front cover. I use MS Word to generate the pages.

Let's look at the cost savings:

- no fee for a back cover
- no fee for a book designer to design the text of the book
- no larger fee for editing and proofreading of 280 pages of a paperback book.

Then I post the ebook on Amazon.com and BarnesandNoble.com. I announce the book on Facebook, LinkedIn.com and Twitter—and on my blog—and see if any copies are purchased.

If copies are purchased, I can consider publishing a paperback version and incurring the above fees.

If there are no purchases of the ebook, I retire the project.

2. Preset the safety net

Fear can often paralyze us to the point that we take no action to formulate our marketing campaign. To overcome such paralysis, I use a process I call "preset the safety net." What does this mean? I basically protect myself by putting team members or a system in place *to prevent my falling on my face.* For example, I hire an editor to improve any marketing description that I write. As a result, I do not hesitate to write my first rough draft because my editor functions as a *safety net.*

I know of a number of artists who do not finish projects. Why? Probably they're afraid that the work will be criticized. The truth is no matter how good something is someone will criticize it. The valuable thing to do then is to set up a system so that you actually accomplish *excellent* work. How? Have people you trust act as your safety net. Or in other words, have them watch your back. For example, I do not hesitate to finish a project because I have *formed a safety net* of having three editors and a proofreader on call. With four professionals whom I trust watching my back, I plow forward with each writing project. I avoid procrastinating. I do not let fear get the best of me.

3. Use fear to jumpstart preparation

When I decided to promote my book *Darkest Secrets of Persuasion and Seduction Masters: How to Protect Yourself and Turn the Power to Good,* I was afraid. Afraid tough questions might lead to misunderstandings and even tarnish my professional reputation. Tarnish how? The whole "darkest secrets" brand may seem to some as exploitive, reveling in dark details—quite negative, in other words. Fortunately, I took my fear and used it as my personal jumpstart point for preparation. How? The fear served as a signal that I needed to get ready for radio/television interviews.

So I sought coaching. I hired two media coaches and prepared my answers to tough questions. I also prepared my theme: "Learning countermeasures to dark, manipulative techniques actually helps one become emotionally strong. You avoid vague fears. You develop your capabilities. And then you're able to move forward with positive action to make your dreams come true."

So how can you use fear to jumpstart preparation? Use it as a signal to put effort into becoming prepared. How? Get coaching, study relevant material, and rehearse. This also applies to marketing. With this book, you're studying relevant material. You could also engage a marketing coach or consultant. You can "rehearse" by trying ideas out with a blog article or by asking some questions via Facebook or LinkedIn.com

You'll notice that the above three practices do not make fear vanish. They don't need to. What they aim for is to reduce the impact of fear. Then, you can move forward with your marketing efforts.

* * *

You learned three practices to handle fear. Now, Chip Conley will demonstrate how to overcome anxiety and make your life and business better:

Mastering the Anxiety Equation: A Remedy for Fearful Times
by Chip Conley

Has Anxiety become your middle name? No doubt, we're living through unpredictable times and this is taking a toll on our physical and emotional health. This is becoming most pronounced in the context of the workplace which is having disastrous impacts on employee engagement and such prized qualities as innovation and creativity, which wither in a fear-based corporate habitat. Some of us resort to tribal, "Lord of the Flies" behaviors to get by, while others of us just retreat to our cubicle in hopes that invisibility is our best means of saving our jobs. Somehow, the contagious emotion of fear has eroded our fundamental trust in our co-workers and the company. In the past few years, the Center for Work-Life Policy (according to Bloomberg Businessweek <http://www.businessweek.com/managing/content/jul2009/ca20090724_345099.htm>) says the percentage of Americans who trust their organizational leaders has dropped from 79% to 37%.

The fact is that almost all anxiety can be distilled down to two basic variables: what we don't know and what we can't control. So, the Emotional Equation for Anxiety? ANXIETY = UNCERTAINTY x POWERLESSNESS. You may have heard about the social science experiment in which people were given the choice between an electric shock now that's twice as painful as one they would receive randomly in the next 24 hours. As you can imagine, the vast majority of people chose more pain now as opposed to less pain at some unpredictable time in the near future. Mystery creates anxiety, especially when we feel we have no influence on the situation.

Once you know the emotional building blocks of Anxiety, you can influence them. Take out a piece of paper and label it "The Anxiety Balance Sheet." Create four columns with the first one being a list of what you DO know with respect to this issue that is giving you anxiety. Then, in the second column, write down what you DON'T know. In the third column, list what you CAN influence with respect to this issue and, finally, in the fourth column, write down what you CAN'T influence. Most people's experience of this exercise is enlightening as they have more items in columns one and three (what they do know and what they can influence) than they expected. But, the magic comes from looking at what you don't know and what you can't control. Often, you can move an item from column two to column one by just asking a few knowledgeable people on the subject whether it's regarding your likelihood of a promotion or your job security. And, I've often seen people review column four and realize that they may have a little more influence over some of these items than they'd previously considered.

In sum, the lessons for leaders are simple. Even if you have bad news, it's better than no news. Transparency is the leadership equivalent of giving people that electric shock early. It may be painful, but the uncertainty creates an even more distracting and debilitating environment. And, as a leader, one of the most effective steps you can take in harrowing times is to help your people steer away from what psychologist Martin Seligman calls "learned helplessness."<http://www.authentichappiness.sas.upenn.edu/Default.aspx> Great leaders help their people see how they can directly impact the company's objectives and their own personal goals. The more externally chaotic the world becomes, the more we need sound internal logic, especially when it comes to our emotions.

CHIP CONLEY, Author and Joie de Vivre Founder

In 1987, Chip Conley started his own hospitality company, Joie de Vivre (JDV), and, as CEO for two dozen years, grew it into the second largest boutique hotel company in the United States. At the age of 26 with no industry experience, Chip transformed a seedy 1950s "no-tell motel" into the world-renowned Phoenix Hotel, a legendary rock 'n roll destination catering to the likes of David Bowie, Linda Ronstadt and Nirvana. JDV expanded into a collection of over 35 award-winning hotels, restaurants and spas, with more than 3,000 employees – each property with its own unique theme that inspires guests to experience an "identity refreshment" during their stay. Chip and his company's time-tested techniques and transformational leadership practices have been featured in *The New York Times, TIME, USA Today, Fortune* and *The Wall Street Journal.*

As the preeminent thought leader at the intersection of psychology and business, and a successful practitioner of emotional intelligence at work, Chip shared his unique prescription for success in *PEAK: How Great Companies Get Their Mojo from Maslow.* Based on noted psychologist Abraham Maslow's iconic Hierarchy of Needs theory, PEAK illustrates how business's three key stakeholders – employees, customers and investors – are ultimately motivated by peak experiences that address their higher, unspoken needs. In his latest book, *The New York Times* bestseller, *Emotional Equations: Simple Truths for Creating Happiness + Success,* Chip takes readers from emotional intelligence to emotional fluency – using math as a way to better understand and manage our emotions. Chip's earlier works include *The Rebel Rules: Daring to be Yourself in Business,* and *Marketing That Matters: 10 Practices to Profit Your Business and Change the World.*

After 24 years as JDV's CEO, Chip is now a Strategic Advisor to the company he founded, and a successful author and international speaker for organizations from TED to PIXAR to

GOOGLE. He has been honored with the highest accolade in the American hospitality industry, the coveted ISHC Pioneer award, and the San Francisco Business Times named him the Most Innovative CEO–and JDV the "2nd Best Place to Work"–in the entire Bay Area.

A committed philanthropist, he served on the board of Glide Memorial Church for nearly a decade and currently serves on the Burning Man Project, Esalen Institute, and Youth Speaks boards. He created the San Francisco Hotel Hero Awards and founded the city's Annual Celebrity Pool Toss event, which has raised millions for inner-city youth programs that now thrive in the troubled neighborhood where he launched his first hotel. Chip received his BA and MBA from Stanford University, and was awarded an Honorary Doctorate in Psychology from Saybrook University, where he is the 2012 Scholar-Practitioner in residence.

Chip's website: www.chipconley.com

* * *

Now, we'll continue learning to be skillful with overcoming fear. Dr. Elayne Savage exposes important elements of the process:

Get Out Of Your Own Way – Overcoming Ambivalence and the Fears That Hold You Back

by Elayne Savage, Ph.D.

By its nature, marketing yourself invites Rejection. Big time.

Fear of Rejection is huge, yet it's just a part of the Fear Team: Fear of Failure (evil twin of Rejection). Joined by Fear of Judgments and Criticism, Fear of Success and Fear of Being Visible. Here's a sneaky one which causes so much trouble—the Fear of Disappointment. When you look closely at Disappointment, you'll see it is often Rejection in disguise.

Still, Fear of Rejection is the team leader, the foundation for all the other fears.

For many years I struggled with these fears. There are other voices as well. They become a shouting match in my head:

"I *can* make a difference!" "No you can't!"

"I can!" "No, you can't!"

"I can!" "No, you can't!"

Opposing voices swirl around. "You can't do it! You can't do it!" answered by "Yes, I can! Yes, I can!"

In this haze of confusion, I can't see clearly. Sometimes it feels like I don't have choices. That's when I used to get immobilized.

And What About You?

Have you ever felt this stuck? Unable to make choices? Paralyzed?

Let's sort it out. We can start by looking at that exhausting tug-of-war between those "voices." The clash between the voice of confidence and the voice of doubt is ambivalence. Ambivalent thoughts and feelings have so many variations, and some are so subtle it's easy to miss them. And missing your distinctive signs of ambivalence can be a barrier to attaining your marketing goals.

Ambivalence is natural to all of us. It's the presence of simultaneously conflicting feelings, ideas or wishes competing with each other. It's a tip off that you're ambivalent when you experience uncomfortable inner conflict and can't make a decision.

You feel stuck, like you're straddling a fence. Ambivalence drains your energy, and it can prevent you from taking action with your marketing.

Where Does Ambivalence Come From?

Ambivalence is usually influenced by messages we heard in our early years.

"You're such a dreamer."

"What makes you think you can do that?"

"Who do you think you are?"

Many of us receive admonitions from parents, teachers, or peers. We hear these warnings as rejecting messages. They discount, dismiss and diminish. Over time we come to interpret these warnings as "Be careful." Cautions like these surely aren't conducive to putting yourself out there, which is the essence of marketing.

Putting ourselves out there can bring up all kinds of fears: Fear of Rejection or Failure or Success; Fear of Visibility or Disappointment.

Uncertainty, Confusion, Anxiety

You have probably faced confusion or fear about taking on new marketing challenges. When two internal voices start skirmishing with one another, this conflict leads to uncertainty and confusion.

The confusion creates anxiety, that can cause you to freeze up and become immobilized. This degree of ambivalence surely isn't productive. It takes a lot of energy to deal with these conflicting voices. Wouldn't you rather put your energy into some other activity?

Tips for Taming Ambivalence

By moving past the ambivalence, it's possible to make space for making marketing choices and taking action. Here's how:

1. Give *both* voices a chance to be heard. When you're only listening to one voice you are, in effect, rejecting the

other. You might even encourage the voices to talk to each other. Out loud. Writing to each other works, too. In other words, you'll be giving voice to both sides of the ambivalence. You'll be honoring both voices. One way to do this is to make two lists: a "What I Have to Gain" list and a "What I Have to Lose" list.

2. It's a good guess that it's some type of Fear that is immobilizing you. You can begin to move forward by naming the Fear. Is it Fear of Rejection? Of Failure? Of Success? Of being Visible? Of Disappointment? Of Judgment? Try naming the Fear to yourself. Next, write it down. Then say it out loud. Hearing yourself say it allows you to see it differently and recognize possible options. Or hear yourself by talking out loud to someone else. A marketing coach can be a terrific help here. These steps can lead to a "Wow! I never saw it like this before," experience. (By the way, these fears are not only attached to your early experiences but also to family messages which are passed down from generation to generation. You can be the first one to break free.)

3. Next, approach the Fear with some detachment. I call it "walking alongside yourself." This means stepping back enough to recognize when you may be starting down that old path of doubt and fear. It means providing enough distance from your emotional tug-of-war to create choices.

4. Then, ask yourself, "Do I really want to continue down this path?" Say, "I could retrace my steps and make the *choice* to return to the fork in the road. I *can* go down a different road."

5. You can learn more about your own early messages by asking yourself these questions:

If I put myself "out there," it would mean . . .

If I fail, it would mean . . .

If I succeed, it would mean . . .

Might I feel disloyal to someone? To whom?

If I feel too visible, what might happen?

When conflicting ideas lead to uncertainty and confusion, call a "time-out" with yourself. Step away from the confusion and sort things out. Putting your confusion into words gives it a container and definition. This allows enough room for choices to emerge.

By understanding your barriers, fears and ambivalence you'll be able to see your options more clearly.

This allows you the space to move forward with Full Strength!

Dr. Elayne Savage, The Queen of Rejection (R), is a communication coach and expert on ambivalence, taking things personally and the fear of rejection. A professional member of the National Speakers Association, she is a workshop leader, trainer, and consultant. Her relationship books, *Breathing Room – Creating Space to Be a Couple* and *Don't Take It Personally! The Art of Dealing with Rejection* have been published in 9 languages.

Website: http://www.QueenofRejection.com

Blog: http://TipsFromTheQueenOfRejection.com

You can follow Elayne on Twitter: @ElayneSavage

***

Now, we go from Dr. Elayne's methods to a powerful process to get the word out about your product or service *without* spending money: free publicity. Now, free publicity expert Danek S. Kaus gives us an introduction:

7 Myths About Getting Free Publicity

by Danek S. Kaus

There is a lot of misunderstanding about the nature of

publicity and how to go about getting it. Here are 7 myths that may keep you from getting the free publicity you deserve.

Myth 1. Publicity and advertising are the same. Advertising is exposure that you pay for. You control the exact message and, if you're willing to pay extra, the placement of the ad.

Publicity is free, unless you are working with a publicist. Even so, the cost of hiring one is much less than the cost of advertising, yet it has more value because it is treated as news.

It has much more credibility than advertising. The downside is, you don't control the placement or size of a story.

Also, you don't have control over the exact spin that a journalist will give the story. But if you initiated the process, by contacting the media with a news release, the story will usually be favorable.

Myth 2. You have to know someone. Like anything else in life, it helps if you have contacts on the inside. But they are not necessary. Every day thousands of people without contacts get free publicity in the media.

They are able to do it because they have a real story to tell, not a bunch of hype or disguised advertising, and they sent the media a well-crafted release.

Myth 3. You have to be one of the big guys to get any media attention. Wrong. See Myth 2 above.

Myth 4. You should send your release everywhere. Doing this is counterproductive. You should target your release to the right outlets and the right journalists.

For example, say your company has just released new customer relations software.

Don't buy a giant media list and send it to everyone on it.

Select the business publications and talk shows and the editors of the business sections of newspapers and magazines, as well as business websites, and send your release to them only.

If you have a list that is detailed enough to give you the contact info for individual business reporters, select those who write about software or high tech, not real estate.

Warning: only send the release to one person at a media outlet at a time. If that person turns you down, then it is okay to contact another one.

Myth 5. You should send out lots of press releases. Don't pester journalists with releases about every little thing that happens at your business or organization.

They find it annoying and time consuming. It's like the boy who cried wolf. Send them too many trivial releases and they will stop paying attention. Wait until you have something reasonably important to share with the public.

Myth 6. Bigger is better. Don't write long press releases. Journalists have too many to read. The ideal length is 400 – 600 words.

If you have more to say, you can provide additional items such as a bio (biography), company history or fact sheet. If the release interests journalists, they will then read your supporting material for more information.

Myth 7. You can get publicity if you buy an ad. Except with smaller media outlets and some trade publications, buying an ad will not influence the decision to do a story on you.

With most journalists, telling them that you will buy an ad if they do a story is a turn off and it may make them decide not to do anything at all. Don't drop your advertising if it is working, but don't try to tie it to getting free publicity.

[Myth 6 mentions the press release. Here are Danek's

thoughts on such an important free publicity tool.]

10 Ways to Write a Great Headline

The headline is the most important part of your press release. It's purpose is to entice the journalist into wanting to read more.

A great headline can also be a guide to help you write the release.

Here are some templates you can use; there are many more, to help you craft eye-catching, publicity generating releases. Some of them use the number 10, but you could also use 5,7, etc. Whatever works.

So here they are:

- The Top 10 __________
- The Best __________
- The Worst __________
- The 10 Best Ways to __________
- The Easiest Ways to __________
- Why You Should Always __________
- Why You Should Never __________
- Why You Should Always __________ When You __________
- Why You Should Never __________ When You __________
- 10 Reasons to __________
- 10 Reasons Not to __________
- 10 Questions You Should Ask Before Choosing a __________ (doctor, lawyer, mechanic, school, charity, etc.)

You may notice that there are actually 12 headlines above. You may wonder why, when the title of this post says there are 10. I'm using one of the principles of business success:

Always under promise and over deliver.

The late **Danek S. Kaus** was the author of *You Can Be Famous! Insider Secrets to Getting Free Publicity.* A former journalist, he published hundreds of articles in about 75 newspapers and magazines, as well as dozens of websites and blogs. He helped authors, business owners and others get free publicity in traditional media and online. Kaus was a best-selling author and a produced screenwriter. He adapted books into screenplays for novelists and true story authors.

* * *

In this chapter, we've discussed methods to quiet down your fear:

1. Reduce the downside
2. Preset the safety net
3. Use fear to jumpstart preparation

Using free publicity serves a small business owner well because it's an opportunity to hone your marketing message and avoid spending money.

Points to Remember:

*** Secret #3: People procrastinate because they're afraid of losing money.**

*** Your Countermeasure:**

Take two approaches to quiet down your fear. First, use the Three Methods to reduce fear: 1) Reduce the downside, 2) Preset the safety net and 3) Use fear to jumpstart preparation. Also, use free publicity.

* * * * * *

Secret #4: People procrastinate because they're afraid of getting no results.

People are afraid of receiving "no results." That's not actually possible. You *always* get results. Some results you like; some you don't. But all of the results provide you with data. You can act on this data and refine your next marketing campaign.

Here's another advantage you gain with each marketing campaign: You have the opportunity to position your business. A number of authors define positioning as a process in which marketers create an identity or image (of a product, brand or organization) in potential customers' minds.

A Case History of Positioning

Positioning is often described as a process in which a marketer creates an identity or image in the minds of targeted customers—also known as the target market.

Positioning often comes down to a few words, like the title of the product. With just a couple of words, you can change the whole perception of said product. For example, some time ago, I viewed a friend's manuscript-in-progress, her proposed book on marketing. I said, "I can co-author the book with you, and we can call the book *Get 'Em to Buy.*"

About a day later, she said a resounding, "No!"

"Why?" I asked. She said the people she talked with labeled the title *Get 'Em to Buy* as "crass." And she did *not* want her name on a book with that title. What title did we settle on? *Full Strength Marketing.* (A useful book, by the way, available on Amazon.com with 21 guest authors and a full description of 10 hidden strengths you can use to make marketing an easier process to experience.)

The question that arises is: "Why was there such a big negative reaction to the title *Get 'Em to Buy*?"

Frankly, I was surprised at the big negative reaction. My first thought was to punch through the noise of modern culture and *get small business owners' attention with that title.*

What's on small business owners' minds? They're certainly concerned about getting business and keeping their company viable. This might be embodied in an old phrase that goes: "Nothing happens until a sale is made." Therefore, a small business owner is vitally concerned with helping people purchase her products or services.

Still, my co-author had been shaken by comments she heard centered on "crass." *The Merriam-Webster Dictionary* defines *crass* as "indicating grossness of mind" and "guided by or indicative of base or materialistic values."

Fair enough. I said to my co-author, "We can soften the title by carefully designing the subtitle to demonstrate that we hold the values of serving customers and bringing good benefits into those customers' lives."

What kind of subtitle could we have used? Perhaps, something like: "Capture Your Target Market's Attention and Serve Them Well." Okay. That subtitle is not good enough. But you can see the intention behind it.

Still, my co-author balked at the *Get 'Em to Buy* title. So how did the situation resolve?

What was the final title of the book? *Full Strength Marketing: How You Can Use Your Hidden Strengths, Break Through Inner Barriers and Raise Your Profits.*

What is really underneath the process of titling a book? Positioning.

In his book, *Crossing the Chasm,* Geoffrey Moore identified a positioning statement, which follows this pattern:

"For (target customer) who (statement of the need or opportunity), the (product name) is a (product category) that (statement of key benefit—that is, compelling reason to buy). Unlike (primary competitive alternative), our product (statement of primary differentiation)."

So what was my co-author objecting to? Her *own* concept of a possible bad position of a book entitled *Get 'Em to Buy*. What elements might form a bad position? To explore them, let's run the positioning model:

A <u>fictional view</u> of a "position" that the "Get 'Em to Buy" title might inspire in a few people. (Notice how this position could relate to my co-author's fears about the "Get 'Em to Buy" title):

"For money hungry businesspeople who just want to get people's cash, *Get 'Em to Buy* is a shallow book that provides manipulative techniques. Unlike wholesome books that provide a holistic approach to serving customers, *Get 'Em to Buy* provides mercenary techniques to merely separate people from their money."

The above is a *fictional* position. Still, consider how much upset can arise from just four words "Get 'Em to Buy." If these ideas were running through my co-author's mind, no wonder she had an allergic reaction to "Get 'Em to Buy."

However, I had a *completely different viewpoint*. Why? I thought that the book could use an attention-getting title and then with the right subtitle, the book would still be perceived as starting from the inspiration of service and helping people. So here are *my* first thoughts as to the position of the book:

"For savvy business people who want to really help others by getting their valuable products into millions of people's hands, *Get 'Em to Buy* is a no-nonsense, powerful book that provides ways to overcome procrastination and other inner blocks so that good people can do marketing well and efficiently. Unlike many marketing books that simply list techniques like an encyclopedia, *Get 'Em to Buy* helps good and helpful business owners overcome their inner blocks and get out there to help their customers!"

And in the above positioning statement, you can see the inspiration for my suggested subtitle: "Capture Your Target Market's Attention and Serve Them Well."

Another possible subtitle could be: "How to Help Your Customers Recognize the Value of Your Product or Service and Enjoy Big Benefits."

My reason for sharing details about the positioning of the title *Get 'Em to Buy* is for us to use it as a useful example of boldness in marketing. **Often, good marketing requires boldness.** You may have noticed an air of regret that I have for not using the *Get 'Em to Buy* title. In fact, I chose to write my next book *without* a co-author to hold me back.

Why does good marketing require boldness? You must first rise above the noise of your competitors, who all screech and attempt to capture your target market's attention. Will you offend some people no matter what you title a product? Probably. If that's true, you need to be bold in your decisions, anyway.

Now, here's an example that I feel good about: I was bold enough to title one of my books, *Darkest Secrets of Persuasion and Seduction Masters: How to Protect Yourself and Turn the Power to Good*. From the moment this title came to my thoughts, I felt it would be a winner. My family members advised against it. But I followed my intuition.

But still I felt uneasy. When I first prepared to be interviewed on radio for my book, I was deeply concerned. I certainly wanted to avoid listeners thinking that the book was exploitative.

As I mentioned earlier, I worked with two media coaches

and developed my answers to tough questions like: "Isn't this *Darkest Secrets* material negative and pushy?" Part of my prepared answers included: "The book is about helping people be emotionally strong. I provide countermeasures to people so that they can handle manipulative techniques thrown at them. When they know they have the tools, they feel capable. And then they can feel strong and fulfill their personal dreams."

Do you notice how I positioned the book? I used vivid words like "emotionally strong," "countermeasures," and "can handle manipulative techniques." Finally, I turn the conversation with the radio show host to the positive "fulfill their personal dreams."

Remember, positioning is a process in which a marketer creates an identity or image in the minds of their target market. I shared the process of titling a book. We saw how a few words can be an essential part of positioning. Focus on the essence of your product. Look for a way to punch through the noise raised by your competition. And consider being bold—if appropriate.

* * *

Above, we discussed positioning; now we'll explore ways to overcome procrastination. If you fear getting "no results" or bad results, use the following process to scale down the risk.

9 Minute Method (#4): Scale Down the Risk / Set a Recovery Plan from the Expenditure

Why You Need to Do This:

Fear can paralyze you unless you take action to assure yourself with a plan to minimize risk. Another part of strengthening your resolve employs a second plan so that you can recover from a cash expenditure on marketing.

First, you'll answer questions related to "Scale Down the Risk." In a moment, I'll ask you to take about five minutes for each of two sets of questions. The idea is for you to brainstorm your answers quickly. Sure, you'll probably refine your answers later. But the point is to help you overcome procrastination by taking small steps *now:*

Scale Down the Risk

1) How can you scale down the risk?

- Example: Send a targeted direct mailing to 1,000 carefully selected people instead of to a list of 5,000 more random ones.
- Example: Use LinkedIn.com and Facebook.com as vehicles to build your list (no cash outlay). Do a Google search to find articles on how you can invite connections in a manner that people find appropriate and not too forward.

2) How can you test elements of your marketing campaign for free?

- Examples: I can write a blog article and see how many people forward it on Facebook. I can come up with two titles for a book and get feedback from past customers.

Now, we'll take about five minutes to answer the following questions:

Set a Recovery Plan from the Expenditure

1) How long will it take you to replace the amount you intend to invest in a marketing campaign?

2) Can you reduce the cost of the marketing campaign? Is it possible to do something valuable with a modest budget?

Can you identify how many freelance jobs you'd need to recover the full amount?

In nine minutes, you have the beginning of two reasonable plans so that you're taking an appropriate risk.

* * *

Now that you have used the 9-minute Method to quiet down fear, use the following methods from Patricia Fripp and David Garfinkel to ramp up your marketing.

How to Market your Way out of Tough Times
by Patricia Fripp & David Garfinkel - one of Fripp's secret weapons!

There's gloom and uncertainty in the air, and most businesses are making a terrible mistake right now in their efforts to ride out the tough times. They're cutting back on marketing and waiting until the economy improves.

In an economy like this, cutting back on marketing is flirting with business suicide. What you should do instead is increase your marketing without increasing the amount of money you spend. This will not only protect you from sales declines, but will also strengthen your business against the threat of deep-pocketed competitors, who may see tough times as a great opportunity to outmaneuver you and grab some of your customers.

How do you get more marketing bang for fewer marketing bucks? By using proven lower-cost, higher-yield methods. Here are five sure cures for marketing woes in tough times:

1. Get back in touch with old customers. It's all too easy to ignore your old customers, but they are often your best source for new business. Sometimes sending a personal note,

making a phone call or inviting an old customer to lunch is all it takes to rekindle a business relationship.

If you want to do this through direct mail or email, you can give old customers a special "Welcome Back" offer—a freebie, a discount, or a bonus when they resume doing business with you.

2. Offer prospective customers a free sample. This is an obvious but often overlooked strategy that certainly can work for your business. Everyone from grocery stores (who offer tidbits of food) to high priced consultants (I spoke to one last week who snared a $10,000 personal coaching client by offering a free first hour) can use this strategy effectively. Don't think it will work in the corporate world? Hmmm... ever hear of a company called AOL?

3. Focus your advertising. Many businesses think "keeping your name in front of the public" is a valid advertising strategy. It's questionable at best, but it's way too risky and low-yield in tough times. Instead, make sure your advertising is only in publications that reach your best prospects, and—this is the most important part—make a specific offer and call to action to get readers of the ad to call you.

One of my clients used this strategy and progressed from 10 lukewarm leads that wouldn't turn into customers, into signed contracts with 35 customers representing millions of dollars worth of business.

4. Let your customers help you out. Business is always a two-way street. Some of your customers who you've helped in the past will be glad to return the favor. Often, all you have to do is ask. Two things you can ask for: testimonials and case studies you can use in your sales presentations and advertising.

Another way they can help you: by giving you referrals.

And if you have an influential customer who's appreciative of what you've done, ask that customer to write and send an endorsed letter to others recommending your business. Offer to pay for the printing and postage, and help with the writing if necessary.

5. Give extra attention to high-integrity behavior. If you think you're the only one who's a little nervous about a lot of things right now, you're not alone. Recent tragic events have increased feelings of distrust across the board. To set yourself apart in the marketplace, go out of your way to conduct business in an especially trustworthy manner. Bend over backwards to be fair about refunds and exchanges.

Do all you can to act in your customers' best interest, even if it means referring them to a competitor (if you don't think you're the best choice for what they want). High-integrity actions can hurt a little in the short-term, but payback is remarkably quick and well worth any sacrifice you may have had to make. If you get (or strengthen) a reputation for being trustworthy, that can be the most precious marketing asset of all in the times ahead.

This is also a great time to invest in sales training. If you would like to know more about how Patricia Fripp can help, email pfripp@fripp.com or see everything you need to make an educated decision on www.fripp.com. Hundreds of companies can't be wrong!!!

David Garfinkel has been described as "the world's greatest copywriting coach." He's a successful results oriented copywriter and the author of *Advertising Headlines That Make You Rich*, which shows you exactly how to adapt proven moneymaking headlines to your business. Find out more about David Garfinkel here:http://www.davidgarfinkel.com

Patricia Fripp, CSP, CPAE is a San Francisco-based executive speech coach and award-winning professional speaker on Change, Customer Service, Promoting Business, and Communication Skills. Fripp offers fresh, usable ideas on getting, keeping and deserving customers. She is Past-President of the National Speakers Association, author of *Get What You Want!*, *Make it So You Don't Have to Fake It* and numerous video and audio programs on presentation skills, marketing, sales, customer service, leadership, team building and more! Meetings and Conventions magazine calls Patricia "one of the country's 10 most electrifying speakers." Her clients include IBM, Sears, Merrill Lynch, Pfizer and American Payroll Association. www.Fripp.com

* * *

After exploring Patricia Fripp and David Garfinkel's comments, we are going to use titling a book as a case study. Coming up with titles for products is both art and science. Here are Ezra Barany's methods:

3 Steps to a Good Book Title That Sells

By Ezra Barany

I must admit, I'm struggling. This struggling makes me feel like not eating my ice cream. I'm working on a sequel to my bestselling thriller *The Torah Codes* and my method for coming up with a good title has turned up zero possibilities.

So why listen to me? Because my method is working. I used the same method to title *The Torah Codes,* a book that is being stumbled upon across the globe! And what my method is successfully telling me is that all my ideas for titles are no good.

The idea of struggling to come up with a single title might come as a surprise to you. Maybe you think the problem is that there are so many possibilities and the difficulty is choosing one. But the reality is there's only one good title for your book.

That good title is the one that makes it easiest for readers who have never heard of you or your novel to find your book. If you just make sure your title fits all three elements your book is bound to be found.

The three required elements are:

1) The title must be relevant to your book;

2) The title is a keyword or phrase often searched in Google and in Amazon; and

3) The title, when put in the Google and Amazon search engines, does not have much competition among the search results.

A Relevant Title

Brainstorm as many possible titles as you can. Try to reach fifty. Figure out the major themes of your book, the lessons to be learned, the location, the traits of your characters, anything and everything that relates so that when the reader reads your book, she'll say to herself, "Oh, yeah! That's why it's titled that." But here's something that's important. Do not have the title be composed of words that are too unknown nor too common. You want phrases that people will type in a search engine.

For my thriller *The Torah Codes,* the main themes were Bible codes and the Shekinah (the female aspect of God). I created a list of possible titles like "The Bible Codes," "The Torah Codes," "Shekinah," "Shekhina," "Shekhinah," (transliterations have different spellings) and so on.

For my sequel, where *The Bourne Identity* meets *The Sixth Sense,* the main themes are the Jewish legend of the 36 righteous, the question of why bad things happen to good people, and the challenge of fighting one's inner demons.

The truth is I haven't done the first step for this book of making a list of titles. That's probably why I'm struggling so much. Instead, I've been brainstorming ideas without writing them down. Ideas like "The 36," "The 36 Righteous," "When Bad Things Happen to Good People," "Fighting Inner Demons," "Jacob Wrestles an Angel," "Wrestling an Angel," and so on. So don't be like me. Instead, write all your ideas down.

The Title as a Coveted Keyword

The question to ask is "Which title is the most searched term on Google every month?" Go to Google's Adwords Keyword tool: https://adwords.google.com/o/Targeting/Explorer?__c=1000000000&__u=1000000000&ideaRequestType=KEYWORD_IDEAS and type in all of your titles.

When you click on the search button, you'll get the results on how many people search your term locally and how many search your term globally. For now, ignore the competition column. When I did a search for my first book, "bible codes" got the most searches, currently at 60,500 global searches a month. Second to that was "Torah codes," at 49,500 global searches a month.

For my second book, none of the terms brought search results higher than 1,000 global searches a month. And you want something between 10,000 to 100,000 global searches a month*. So I looked beneath my search results to the list of related search terms. Scanning those gave me some ideas. There's already a book, similar to mine, called *The Righteous Men* with 9,900 global searches monthly. It's not 10,000 but it's close enough. If I titled mine *The 36 Righteous Men,* then I'd be able to ride the coat tails of that other thriller.

From the looks of it, most of the searches for "The

Righteous Men" are specifically targeted to find that other thriller, "The Righteous Men." Do I feel guilty for taking away his book sales? No! Because I'll actually be helping his book sales! When I promote my book, people who look up "The 36 Righteous Men" will also find his book, so it's a win-win situation. Seems like The 36 Righteous Men is a good title.

So maybe my method worked after all.

The Title With Little Competition

Now that you have narrowed down your brainstorm list to three or four highly-searched keywords for your title, make sure there's only one to three other websites or books that use those titles. Ideally, zero is best. You can check the competition column in the Google Adwords Keyword tool to see if your title has low, medium, or high competition. Once you confirm they have low competition, go to Amazon and do a search for your three or four possible titles.

When I did a search for "The Bible Codes," a ton of books came up. In the Google search engine, there were also tons of websites about Bible codes. When I checked "The Torah Codes," no books came up and very few websites came up in Google. I clearly found a winning title!

I made a website called www.TheTorahCodes.com to make the Google search term come straight to me, and on Amazon my book is at the top of the search results. When you find that unique (low competition) and often-searched book title, be sure to set up a website whose URL is the title of your book. Then, once your book is published, congrats! You've set up a great system for people to easily stumble upon your book! Now you can eat ice cream.

*I gleaned this information from a lecture by RC Peck.

Book marketing mentor, **Ezra Barany** is the author of the award-winning bestseller, *The Torah Codes*,

http://www.amazon.com/Torah-Codes-Ezra-Barany/dp/0983296014/. Contact Ezra today to begin the conversation on how he can help you now via Facebook, https://www.facebook.com/ezra.barany

Twitter, https://twitter.com/suspenseauthors or contact him through this blog, or email: EZRA at THETORAHCODES.COM.

* * *

In this chapter, we have discussed positioning and even have looked at titling books as a case study. Remember, you need to connect with your intended audience so that you can craft your product titles so they are both enticing and compelling.

Points to Remember:

*** Secret #4: People procrastinate because they're afraid of getting no results.**

*** Your Countermeasure:**

Use the Positioning Model. Craft a position statement using this template: "For (target customer) who (statement of the need or opportunity), the (product name) is a (product category) that (statement of key benefit—that is, compelling reason to buy). Unlike (primary competitive alternative), our product (statement of primary differentiation)."

* * * * * *

Secret #5: People procrastinate because they don't know where to begin.

In marketing, the discussion often begins with your target

market. Who is your customer? How do you want to help them?

On the other hand, some people begin with a "cool idea." But they can fall down by failing to find people who really want or need such a "cool product." There's an old phrase: "Inventing a cure for no known disease." Having a cool idea is not enough. You need to identify a particular group of people who would cheer to have your product improve their lives.

One way to start a business is to identify people whom you want to work with and then to ask: "Where are they hurting?" Business builds on solving problems and providing benefits. What kind of benefits? How about consolidating much of one's personal tech equipment? Many of us remember in 2007 at MacWorld, when Steve Jobs said, "Well, today, we're introducing three revolutionary products of this class. The first one is a widescreen iPod with touch controls. The second is a revolutionary mobile phone. And the third is a breakthrough Internet communications device. So, three things: a widescreen iPod with touch controls; a revolutionary mobile phone; and a breakthrough Internet communications device. An iPod, a phone, and an Internet communicator. An iPod, a phone … are you getting it? These are not three separate devices, this is one device, and we are calling it iPhone. Today, Apple is going to reinvent the phone, and here it is."

Were people hurting before the iPhone arrived? Maybe not. But I know several people who would feel lost without their iPhone now!

So zero-in on the benefits you want to provide and the people you want to serve. These are your customers—that is, your target market.

Discover Your Target Market

Sometimes your best target market is yourself. Or perhaps, your younger self. The one who understood less than you do now. For example, one of my books with consistent sales every month is *Darkest Secrets of Making a Pitch for Film and Television.* I cannot tell you how much I wish that book had been in my hand twenty years ago.

Consider what you know now that you wished you knew ten years ago or even two years ago. You might find that you have a product idea that can really serve others. For example, I notice that many professional speakers write books on public speaking because they have hard-won wisdom they gained on their way up.

Other times, you come up with a vague idea for a product for other people. Who is your product for? This seems like a simple question—yes? Actually, it's the tip of the iceberg.

What you really need is a series of questions to take a vague idea and convert it into something truly specific and useful.

Write down these ten questions and come up with first draft answers. Don't hesitate as you take a first pass at these questions. Just go with your gut feelings. You might discover surprising insights into who you want to serve and what you know about them.

1) Who is the product/service for?
2) How long have they been in business or in their current career?
3) What is a big problem they face?
4) How do they feel because of this problem?
5) What is the "salve" I am offering to them?
6) What would stop them from buying my product?
7) Tell me more. How is life going for them?
8) What is their age?

9) How do I know they'll respond positively to my product?
10) What transformation do they want? [Perhaps they want to feel more confident or gain new skills or free themselves from some drudgery.]
11) How can I demonstrate that I'm trustworthy to them?

Use these questions as a springboard to help you further define your target market.

* * *

Now we'll explore the essence of marketing.

Marketing Is Trust

Good marketing gains trust. How do you do that?

Tell a story. Why?

If you say, "Best customer service in the country," the prospective customer reflexively thinks: "Oh yeah? Prove it."

But if you tell a story, it slips under the radar. How does that happen? Researchers theorize that it is because we are raised on stories as children. Every moment across the world, children are saying, "Tell me a story."

One of the most successful marketing websites I ever wrote began with:

Dear Reader,

I never expected to write *Darkest Secrets of Persuasion and Seduction Masters: How to Protect Yourself and Turn the Power to Good*. But I was angry and I had to stand up for you.

When I was a child, I was hurt badly. My parents could not protect me. As a young man, in one of my first business deals, I was hurt terribly.

Now, I'm 44 years old, with gray in my hair, and for 24 years I have been taking action to protect people.

And now is the time that I protect you with the countermeasures I reveal in *Darkest Secrets of Persuasion and Seduction Masters.*

Every human being needs to be able to break the trance that a manipulator will create. You need to make good decisions so you are safe and growing and not cut off at the knees.

This *Darkest Secrets* material is so intense that I am only releasing it by counterbalancing it with my most energizing and uplifting books *10 Seconds to Wealth* and *Nothing Can Stop You This Year!*

Now it's time, this very minute, for me to write this to protect you. I must speak the truth.

These darkest secrets of persuasion masters are … Wait a minute. Let's say it plainly: These are the darkest secrets of masters of manipulation.

— — — —

As you can see, tell a story and you do four effective things: arouse curiosity, create tension, use suspense and prove the triumph. These four elements provide a good story.

And in effective marketing the fifth element is "Ask for the order" (that is, ask the person to buy).

Now you're on your way to Effective Marketing.

* * *

Now, we'll use a process to help you brainstorm ideas for a powerful story you can use to inspire your buyers to purchase your product/service.

9-Minute Method (#5): Three Circles Process

Why You Need to Do This:

Earlier in this section, we did a process to help you identify your target market. One of the ways to really move your target market to purchase your product/service is to use a powerful story. You'll identify benefits that your target market will enjoy, and upon that foundation you'll zero-in on useful stories for your marketing campaign.

We'll now do some brainstorming. I'll demonstrate the process, and then later you'll do the exercise. The purpose of the following Three Circles Process is to help you get ideas on paper quickly and to see connections. From your brainstorming on paper, you can begin focusing on useful stories to move the hearts and minds of your target market.

Step 1: Draw three circles.

Step 2: Label the circles: Product/Service, Benefits for Target Market, My Personal Stories.

Step 3: Write quickly and place appropriate ideas into each of the circles.

Now, I'll share my example:

Circle #1: Product/Service

My book *Darkest Secrets of Negotiation Masters.*

Circle #2: Benefits for Target Market

- Discover dark techniques people use to get the upper hand in a negotiation.
- Learn countermeasures to protect oneself from such tricky methods.
- Handle negotiation with calm and poise.
- Avoid being taken in by manipulative methods.

Circle #3: My Personal Stories

- My story of standing up against a clerk and a supervisor who were selling poor jewelry to a family member
- My story of dealing with someone's email that read, "The negotiation is over."

The Exercise:

In a moment, I'll invite you to do those three steps. The purpose is for you to identify important elements upon which you can build your marketing campaign. In Circle #3, you could write down stories of past clients who have had outstanding results using your product or service.

Step 1: Draw three circles.

Step 2: Label the circles: Product/Service, Benefits for Target Market, My Personal Stories.

Step 3: Write quickly and place appropriate ideas into each of the circles.

Your goal is to ultimately identify five stories and settle on two that feel promising. You can build your marketing campaign on a foundation of a good story (as you saw with my above example: the story that I used for my website for *Darkest Secrets of Persuasion and Seduction Masters*).

* * *

Good marketing calls for good stories. Now Gayl Murphy helps you refine your approach. You'll learn about "pitching."

You Gotta Pitch It to Promote It so You Can Tell It to Sell It!

by Gayl Murphy

"Your business pitch" is what's left standing after you've

left the building. Fit the problem AND the solution in your pitch, and you've got them at "hello." You don't have to make your pitch perfect, you just have to nail it in "five seconds or less!"

Creating and delivering your business pitch is about who you are, what you do and what's next. This extremely effective networking tactic can often feel a lot like online dating to a newbie, like cyber lovers scouring the web in search of a special connection—it can be terribly daunting if you don't know what you're doing.

That said, when you are dating online, if you don't post a picture (preferably current), you won't get many dates because "one picture tells a thousand words", just like a "Killer Pitch can make you millions!" You've got to make that connection in an instant so people can "see you in action" just by meeting you.

A Killer Pitch can get you connected and in the door, clean and simple. Meaning, a good pitch will get you a two to three minute conversation; a Killer Pitch will book you a lunch with them walking you to your car!

An Elevator Pitch is about who you are and what you're selling. And, an "Interview Tactics! Killer Pitch" is whatever you need it to be in whatever environment you happen to be in at anytime. Making it the right tool for the right time!

Let's set the record straight right here and right now, you can have as many pitches for your business as you want. This is great news for those of you whose businesses are diversified over several markets. You can have a killer pitch that's three seconds, 30 seconds, 90 seconds, or three minutes.

With Interview Tactics!, you can create lots of different pitches so you can adequately decide which pitch you think is most appropriate to use, depending on who you're talking to and where you are. It's called knowing your end-user and being target-specific. Again, it's the right tool for the right time. The key to this is really asking a few questions of the person you're talking to so you can best choose the right one, so as to make what you're selling about them.

For example, when I'm networking with CEOs, one of my pitches is, "I celebritize CEO's", which is a terrific attention grabber with head honchos, and they always want to know more. When I'm at Book Expo, I want to be just as specific with authors, so my pitch is "I celebrit-ize authors." And, when I'm at the Inventor's Expo, I pitch that "I celebrit-ize inventors." And I do all of the above. The funny thing is that it's the same job for all three, with a bit of tailoring.

You can and should be just as flexible with your pitching when your customer base is diversified. Think of the Hollywood Dry Cleaner. He cleans all the clothes in show business and they all need him, regardless of how diversified their businesses are. So he can brand himself as the Dry Cleaner to the Stars, the Studio Executive's Dry Cleaner, or George Clooney's Stylists Dry Cleaner! Guess what? His job is exactly the same regardless of whose dirt he shouts out.

Think about all the different markets your business serves and start expanding who you pitch to. Can you have a separate pitch for stay at home moms, seniors, astronauts, students, families, solopreneurs, reinvented entrepreneurs, scientists, insurance salesmen? You get the picture.

As for me, when I'm coaching or speaking about "Interview Tactics!" my job never changes, but my end-users do, so I stay keenly aware of all the businesses and markets that might need what I'm selling at any time, so I can pitch to them, too.

In my experience, the very best pitches are the ones that

sell themselves. Meaning that they're easily repeatable, full of color and detail, visual, direct, concise and solidly to the point.

A "Killer Pitch" is so engrossing that people become compelled to move it forward for you, word for word, especially if it's clever. You can create pitches that literally sell themselves by being target specific. For example, everyone wants more time. How about instead of telling customers that they'll save time with your product, why not tell them exactly how much more time they'll have as a result of working with you? Do the math in advance and give them examples of extra time over the period of six weeks.

Or, who doesn't want to lose weight? By creating a Killer Pitch for your "Get Skinny Fast Diet," you can not only show people how to lose weight fast, but by following your directions they'll be 20 pounds lighter in 30 days. You're giving them a roadmap so they know what to expect and they can see the results of their hard work.

By being specific, you not only give your end-user a personalized message, you're also writing their script so they know how to comfortably pitch you to their friends, family, co-workers and the next person they meet. Or, even better, they can tell their boss exactly what you do and how terrific you really are, word for word.

Questions to self for creating "The Power Pitch":

- What problem does my business solve?
- Does it save my end-user time or money? If so, how?
- Will it make my end-user more money? How?
- Will it make them happier? Healthier? Younger? Sexier? Thinner? (You need to know how for all of these.)

- Will it buy them more time to play and be sociable? Spend more time with friends and family?
- Will they learn something of great benefit to their lives and the lives of their community or country? (Hint: This is important if your product is a charity, or on a medical, health/wellness or green topic.)
- Can your business, product or service jump-start their business?

It's important that you have at least two or three answers to each of these questions so you always have scenarios and examples about your business available to tell anyone at anytime.

One great way to stay on top of information about your area of expertise is by subscribing to Google Alerts. Google Alerts can be found on Google.com. When you subscribe, Google will send you an email every day, or weekly, listing all the internet chatter on your topic for that day or week.

Be sure to input your keywords and core message for maximum results. Your Google Alert will include the latest breaking news, the latest studies and the newest innovations in your field. This will keep you at the top of your game and ahead of the competition. You'll be such a know-it-all. Creating commonality with the person you're talking to is also a huge benefit, meaning taking what you do and relating it to everyday things that we all experience and think about. By breaking your business down in this way, you're actually expanding the base of your business and making your products available to a lot more people than you think. Remember, people have people.

Gayl Murphy is a Media Entrepreneur on a mission. Get the story; get it right and coach entrepreneurs to craft media messages that make millions! Gayl is a veteran Hollywood Correspondent,

Media and Presentational Coach, Speaker and Author of *Interview Tactics! How to Survive the Media without Getting Clobbered!* As a Media Expert Gayl celebritizes entrepreneurs in business and entertainment to successfully use media to celebritize themselves and their brands, so they can pitch it to promote it and tell it to sell it ... anytime, any place. As a Showbiz correspondent, Gayl interviews the stars! She's interviewed over 15,000 of the biggest celebrities and newsmakers in the world on radio, TV and in print for ABC News, BBC News, SKY News, E! and HollywoodToday.net among others. InterviewTactics.com
Gayl@InterviewTactics.com 01-323-417-5172

* * *

Now that Gayl Murphy introduced you to facets of pitching, how can you begin marketing your message without spending money? Use free online marketing. Danek S. Kaus reveals Twitter strategies.

Free Publicity with a Huge Twitter Following
by Danek S. Kaus

By now you probably realize how powerful Twitter can be for marketing. In order for Twitter to be truly effective, you will need to have a lot of followers. Here's how:

1. Create a great Twitter bio. One of the key factors in whether or not people decide to follow you is the quality of the information in your bio. If you have a relevant website, be sure to include the URL. You only have 160 characters, as opposed to the 140 allowed in tweets, so use them well.

2. If you're new to Twitter, create about 10 or so interesting tweets before looking for followers. You have to give people a reason to want to follow you.

3. Links to interesting websites, articles and videos make great tweets. Because the URLs will be too long for Twitter,

you'll need to create a short version. You can do this at tinyurl.com. Copy the long link and paste it into the appropriate window there and it will generate a short link that is suitable for Twitter.

4. Humorous and inspiring quotes make great tweets and are among the most popular. Lots of sites post great quotes for you to use. Find them with a Google search.

5. Tweet links to interesting videos from YouTube and other such sites.

6. Make sure you re-tweet other people's tweets. Many of them will do the same for you, which exposes you to their followers, some of whom may decide to follow you.

7. Join the conversation. Reply to other people's tweets, give them a compliment or thank them for sharing. These people may also decide to send you @ messages, which will also make their followers aware of you.

8. Be sure to thank people who re-tweet you. All you have to do is hit the reply button and send a short note.

9. Become active on Follow Friday. Each Friday, recommend some of your favorite tweeters to your followers by typing in #FollowFriday or #FF and then their Twitter handle, such as @JaneSmith. Others will do the same for you. This is a great way to get more Twitter Followers.

10. Follow all of Twitter's rules about following and un-following. Don't become too aggressive or your account will be suspended.

11. Limit your marketing tweets. Try to keep a ratio of about one marketing tweet for every 10 regular ones.

12. Use *We Follow*. Type in a key word that relates to your topic, such as parenting. A list of Twitter people with large followings will come up. Follow these people and, more importantly, follow their followers. If you have interesting tweets, about 20 – 30% of them will follow you back. In the

early stages, follow about 100 a day. You don't want to have a too disproportionate ratio of people you are following.

The late **Danek S. Kaus** was the author of *You Can Be Famous! Insider Secrets to Getting Free Publicity*. A former journalist, he published hundreds of articles in about 75 newspapers and magazines, as well as dozens of websites and blogs. He helped authors, business owners and others get free publicity in traditional media and online. Kaus was a best-selling author and a produced screenwriter. He adapted books into screenplays for novelists and true story authors.

* * *

Now, we'll explore better methods of using social media. Elaine Fogel shows the way.

Are You Integrating Social Media to Get More Leads?
by Elaine Fogel

So, your business or nonprofit organization is involved in social media marketing. But, are you capitalizing on it to bring targeted audiences to you?

The ultimate marketing scenario is when your prospects find you. Whether it's by word-of-mouth, a formal introduction or referral, or online, *inbound marketing* [http://www.trustemedia.com/inbound-marketing-definition.html] means several advantages for your organization.

According to a recent *MarketingSherpa study* [http://www.marketingsherpa.com/article.php?ident=32211#], the benefits of integrating social media as part of an inbound marketing strategy are considerable, as the integration empowers organizations to:

- generate relevant content (My comment: VERY IMPORTANT!)
- increase the number of inbound links
- create more relevant listings to show in search engine results pages
- maintain or improve their current rankings for targeted keywords
- make it easier for prospects and customers to find the information they want
- track inbound leads from initial engagement to conversion with standard analytics tools

Yet, even though three-quarters of organizations think that integrating social media with SEO (search engine optimization) is essential, "more than 50% are not involved in inbound marketing or, worse, they don't even know what it is."

In addition, the research "showed a 59% improvement in *conversion rates*

[http://www.marketingterms.com/dictionary/conversion_rate/] from *organic search*

[http://www.marketingterms.com/dictionary/organic_search_results/] traffic for marketers who integrated social media and SEO, over those who did not."

And, since your business or organization's success depends on being found, inbound marketing is something you'll want to know more about. Here are some good resources to get you going:

When It Comes To Inbound Marketing Time Is Definitely Of The Essence (Forbes)

[http://www.forbes.com/sites/marketshare/2012/05/22/when-it-comes-to-inbound-marketing-time-is-definitely-of-the-essence/]

How To Execute Inbound Marketing Campaigns

(Inbound Commerce)
[http://www.ecommerceinboundmarketing.com/how-to-execute-inbound-marketing-campaigns-like-hubspot/]

Why Content is The Cornerstone of Inbound Marketing Success (Business 2 Community)
[http://www.business2community.com/content-marketing/why-content-is-the-cornerstone-of-inbound-marketing-success-0211993]

50 Ideas On How Businesses Can Use Social Media To Increase Visibility And Traffic (Business 2 Community) Great list! [http://www.business2community.com/social-media/50-ideas-on-how-businesses-can-use-social-media-to-increase-visibility-and-traffic-0208154]

Elaine Fogel is a professional speaker and president and CMO of SOLUTIONS Marketing & Consulting LLC, a boutique marketing and communications agency located in Scottsdale, Arizona. From her earlier agency career assignments in Canada freelance copywriting Procter & Gamble, Nestlé Carnation, and Kraft materials, to positions at leading organizations such as Canadian Breast Cancer Foundation and March of Dimes in Canada, Elaine has a strong passion for marketing, communications, branding and customer orientation.

She has been a contributing writer for MarketingProfs.com and The Business Journal and her articles have appeared in many publications, including the *Stanford Social Innovation Review, Marketing News, The Arizona Republic,* I, and several association publications. She has been interviewed by CNN, *Connect Magazine,* and *The Capitol Times,* and her content was included in several books including one of the *Guerrilla Marketing* series.

Company Website: www.solutionsmc.net

Speaking: www.elainefogel.com

Blog: Totally Uncorked on Marketing

http://elainefogel.net

Contact Information: elaine@solutionsmc.net

***

Let's continue with our discussion of online marketing. Now Beth Barany gives us more insights to the use of Twitter.

Promotions on $0 Budget: Use Twitter for a Purpose
By Beth Barany

Twitter is a lot of fun! I'd be the first to admit it. And it's a time suck. In researching this article I spent WAY too much time playing on Twitter, doing good things—which I'll get to later—but it's distracting nonetheless. Lesson: set a time to write the article [done!] and a time limit on Twitter. [I'm going to have to work on that one!]

You may think that using Twitter is a complete waste of time (see above), but actually it's a goldmine of promotional opportunities for authors. If you use Twitter to grow your fan base, build your book buzz, and ultimately sell your books, then Twitter can be worth all your time away from your current work in progress. Yah!

Before We Begin – Twitter Basics

To get started on Twitter, here are the steps:

1. Create a free account and fill out your profile information.
2. Choose a picture, background and bio that stays aligned with your brand.
3. Import your contacts from your email account.
4. Then start searching for your favorite authors, media folks, and interesting people to follow.

In Twitter, who you follow won't necessarily follow you back, though they may. You also don't have to follow those who follow you. I do recommend you follow your fans, once you've identified them. Which leads us to our first main opportunity: grow your fan base.

Grow Your Fan Base

Whether you're a newly published author or have a few books under your belt, Twitter is a great way to have direct and timely contact with your readers. By direct, I mean you can send them a message via Twitter called a direct message or DM for short. Handy, huh?! By timely, I mean right away! Okay, when it's your social networking time.

Regarding DM's, individuals can only send you a direct message if you're following them. So, follow back if you want to use this feature.

You can also write a Twitter post (often called a tweet) directly back to someone and mention them. Everyone likes some Twitter love.

Actual Twitter Example: "@ann_aguirre We'll miss you while you're gone. Enjoy DRAGON AGE".

For as yet unpublished authors, you can use Twitter too! Connect with your potential fan base by chatting (DMing in twitter parlance) with fans of your favorite authors. Share about your favorite authors in the genre in which you write. When it comes time for you to chat about your first book, your fellow fans can get excited about your book and become your fan.

Continue the conversation by occasionally inviting followers to visit your site or blog and sign up for your newsletter, if you have one, or sign up for your RSS feed for your blog.

Build Your Book Buzz

You can build buzz around your book by getting other

people to buzz for you. One way to do this is to talk about other people's books a lot, as does Ann Aguirre, paranormal romance author, https://twitter.com/MsAnnAguirre, and romance author, Bella Andre, http://twitter.com/bellaandre, among many others.

Another way to build buzz is to interact with the buzz builders: book reviewers. By following romance author, Carolyn Jewel's Twitter (@jewel), I found LimeCello (http://twitter.com/limecello), an avid book reviewer who interacts with the authors she reviews and raves over. It was fun to follow her send up of various authors and see them answer back.

Find book reviewers by using Lists, a new Twitter feature that allows you to collect groups of Twitter folks under one, well, list. Anyone can create a list. I'm sure I was not the only one to create one for book reviewers: http://twitter.com/Beth_Barany/book-reviewers. Check out the reviewers' sites to be sure they cover your genre, then engage the right ones in a Twitter conversation.

Book Sales

While it may be difficult to track book sales because of Twitter, you can increase your author platform—the size of your audience—by using Twitter to point out how great and awesome you are! I mean, how your books rock the house. Or, how absolutely smart and snarky you are. Whatever fits your book, your style, and your author brand.

Above all, have fun with Twitter! Interact with new fans, build buzz, and shine a light on your books!

Links mentioned in this article:

List of Book reviewers on Twitter:http://twitter.com/Beth_Barany/book-reviewers

Book reviewer, LimeCello: http://twitter.com/limecello

Romance author, Bella Andre:
http://twitter.com/bellaandre
Romance author, Carolyn Jewel:
https://twitter.com/cjewel
Paranormal romance author, Ann Aguirre:
http://twitter.com/ann_aguirre

First published *The Heart of the Bay,* in the column, the Promotion Posse—a monthly column spotlighting promotional strategies for authors, written by members of SFA-RWA with a knack for PR.

Beth Barany is the bestselling author of *The Writer's Adventure Guide: 12 Stages to Writing Your Book,* and *Overcome Writer's Block: 10 Writing Sparks To Ignite Your Creativity.* Beth speaks to groups and conferences all over the San Francisco Bay Area and across the United States and Europe. Beth Barany is also an award-winning novelist. Her current novel is *Henrietta The Dragon Slayer,* a young adult fantasy novel, available in print and in ebook format. You can connect with her on Twitter and bug her with questions at: https://twitter.com/Beth_Barany. More about Beth and how she helps authors create successful careers at http://www.bethbarany.com.

* * *

If you do not know much about marketing, you would probably do well to hire a couple of contractors. You'll need to lead them. An important part of leadership is listening. Now, Kimberly Gleason reveals vital listening skills.

How to Listen So You Get Results

by Kimberly Gleason

Blah, blah, blah, blah…. It's so easy to talk, to ramble on about our thoughts, our ideas, our concerns, our beliefs, our demands. We are expert ramblers, monopolizers of conversations, hijackers of others' time, often unaware of how we project ourselves, and worse, frequently indifferent to others' views. Listening, on the other hand, not only shows that you value the other person's humanity but also is the key to getting the results you want, whether the result be a change in someone's perspective, an agreement in your favor, or a strengthened relationship.

While we all know the importance of listening, it's easy to forget that there are certain strategies for listening that when implemented will help you to create true dialogue and an increased likelihood of achieving the outcome you seek. Here are seven of those strategies.

Determine what you want.

Determining what you want ahead of time is necessary for conversations that are critical, because you know that one direction or another will lead you either away from or toward your goal. For example, if you decide upfront that you want an enjoyable conversation that results in a closer relationship with a friend or colleague, then you will know to listen for opportunities to share and connect on a similar level. On a parallel note, if you are engaged in conversation with your boss, and you desire a promotion, you will listen with a critical ear in regards to whether it is the right timing, what your boss thinks of you, what he or she values in an employee, what opportunities are available, and what the vision is for the company. Thus, determining what you want will help you to ask the right questions and to listen carefully.

Focus on the other person.

Nobody likes talking to somebody whose eyes glaze over,

lost in his own thoughts, or a person who's fidgeting with her pen. If you want someone to truly feel heard, and consequently understood, then give that person your full attention. Don't become distracted by what else is going on in the room or even by your own opinions. I love the Bible verse in the book of James about being "quick to listen, slow to speak." You will have plenty of time to formulate what you want to say later. Focus and really listen.

Show interest.

Use eye contact to show you've connected to the person speaking. Encourage them to continue speaking by giving an occasional "uh-huh." Smile, nod, laugh. Show that you value what they have to say, and they are more likely to listen to you.

Observe body language.

Someone once said, "If you feel like no one is listening to you, learn a new language." Listen to what's not being said by examining the speaker's body language. And better yet, match theirs. We've all heard how body language, depending on the study, accounts for 80-90 percent of language. Think of the tremendous amount of data you can gather simply by observing gestures, facial expressions, and posture. Is he frowning, smirking, or avoiding eye contact? Is she hunched over as if exhausted and frazzled? When appropriate, match their body language. If you're both sitting at a table and he leans forward while speaking (which generally means he's comfortable with you), then you should lean forward as well to intensify the connection.

Paraphrase what the person said.

Of course you don't want to paraphrase every response of

the person speaking—that would only be annoying. However, it is very appropriate, and useful, to occasionally do so. Paraphrasing helps you to clarify what the other person said, and gives him or her the opportunity to clear up any misunderstandings. Paraphrasing also confirms that you understand, and bottom line—people want to feel understood.

Ask questions.

If you want to achieve results by listening, then ask open-ended questions. Asking open-ended questions (not simply "yes/no" questions) shows the other person that you're interested in what he or she has to say, as well as allows you to gain additional, often vital information prior to your response. The open-ended question is one of the best tools I use with my coaching clients for drawing out the pertinent, revealing information that will help them to ultimately achieve their goals.

Use silence.

Rarely do we enjoy silence in a conversation. We begin to feel flustered, worried that we may bore our audience. So we find ways to fill the gap in dialogue. Using silence, however, encourages the speaker to continue talking, to explore other ideas, to expand on previous ones. Basically, when you allow silence to be a tool at your disposal, you will hear more, and on a deeper level. You prove that you truly care about that person's beliefs, values, ideas, and concerns.

Remember that the key to getting results is not merely to talk, but to listen, and listen well. People want to feel valued, appreciated, respected, and liked. Mostly, they want to feel understood. You can make that happen. If they believe that you regard them in these ways, they are more apt to hear you out. And better yet, when it's your turn, you will know what to say.

Kimberly Gleason is a nationally recognized, board-certified personal and executive leadership coach, author, speaker, and owner of Kimberly Gleason Coaching, a coaching company that partners with leaders, teams, and organizations to overcome their significant challenges and achieve their life, career, and company goals. She specializes in developing leaders' effectiveness, enhancing communication, and building high performing teams. You can find out more about her free e-books, blog, resources, presentations, and programs at

www.kimberlygleasoncoaching.com.

Here's to an adventurous life and career.

Kimberly Gleason, BCC
Kimberly Gleason Coaching
Executive leadership coach, personal coach, and speaker
www.kimberlygleasoncoaching.com
"Flourish and Grow: Your Life, Your Career, Your Leaders"
616-364-7459

* * *

We have covered ways to get started with Twitter and other social media opportunities. Not only do you need to start, you need to keep up your momentum.

How You Can Have Momentum for Your Success

"How did you write 25 books?" a client asked me. My first response was: "I protect my momentum." Here's how you can create success, using the F.L.O.W. plan:

F – Follow your heart

L – Let people know

O – Open a logbook

W – Wrangle some space

1. Follow your heart

Many of us are so busy that our small voice from our heart is silenced. What do you want? Do you want to write a story or a novel? Do you want to make a short film? Do you want to paint or act? Pause. Write on a sheet of paper the answers to these questions: "What are your secret wishes? What would you do if you could not fail?"

2. Let people know

Tell family and friends that you are protecting your momentum. You'll likely need to explain it. And, just because you say it, don't expect that you'll be free of resistance. Let's face it. If one parent usually makes dinner, then the kids and the other parent probably like the status quo. Loved ones just need to adapt to the new pattern. Tell your loved ones that you need their support. And make it worth their effort. Tell them how you'll reward them and you–for your accomplishing what you're aiming for. Provide such rewards for incremental success. If you decide to write 200 words a day, reward yourself and your loved ones after five days of diligent work.

3. Open a logbook

I log how many words I write per day. For example, for one of my upcoming books I just completed 34,835 words. Why does keeping a log help? It's a way of celebrating and it's a way of personally patting yourself on the back. Don't wait for the world to be proud of you. Keep a log and be proud of yourself. Feel the rush of knowing in your bones that you're making progress.

4. Wrangle some space

The Merriam-Webster Dictionary defines wrangle as "to herd and care for (livestock and especially horses) on the range" or "to obtain by persistent arguing or maneuvering." I'd prefer to *drop* the arguing part. However, the "maneuvering" part is necessary. People like to get their way. So get clever. Make a deal. In return for loved ones' support of you keeping up your momentum, make a plan with them to celebrate your diligent efforts.

Momentum is precious. Whether I start with an idea for a book and then have it completed 70 days later or I work on a screenplay over one year, I know that I will log my progress and enjoy each milestone I reach.

Be sure to guard your momentum. Some people get on a roll and feel too confident and stop. No! Keep on going when you have the momentum (three important details: eat, exercise and get enough sleep).

Some people get stuck in goals that are about survival (getting out of debt or losing weight). Others get excited about goals that "pull them forward." These are the life-energizing goals. These are the goals that unleash your creativity.

When you get some momentum, keep it up.

You'll live the life of your dreams!

* * *

Remember you might be procrastinating because you do not know where to begin. So what's your assignment? Find ways to discover how to begin. We have discussed ways to get started with Twitter and other forms of social media. We even covered how to maintain your momentum. Start today.

Points to Remember:

*** Secret #5: People procrastinate because they don't know where to begin.**

*** Your Countermeasure:**

Begin by answering questions about your target market (see the questions in the chapter). Then look into sharing your marketing message for free through social media. Use Twitter and more. Start small. Be consistent. (I write a *weekly* blog article and announce it on Twitter, Facebook and LinkedIn. You can do the same.)

* * * * * *

Secret #6: People procrastinate because they don't know how to do marketing.

When many of us confront marketing for the first time or twentieth time, it's a daunting task, one that can seem insurmountable. We throw up our hands and say, "Oh, no. I don't know where to start. Ugh, I could screw this up!" First of all, we need to discover what people really want and what truly motivates them to buy.

What Do People Really Want? And How Can You Get 'Em to Buy?

What is the "holy grail" that marketers, for hundreds of years, have been reaching for? It's the real reason people buy.

Many theories of people's true desires have arisen. Here are a few:

Psychologists at the University of Rochester conducted research about what keeps video game players playing. The researchers discovered that video games provided opportunities for achievement, freedom, and even a connection to other players. Lead investigator in four studies, psychologist Richard M. Ryan said, "It's our contention that the psychological 'pull' of games is largely due to their capacity to engender feelings of autonomy, competence, and relatedness."

Blair Warren, known as a "master influencer," wrote: "People will do anything for those who encourage their dreams, justify their failures, allay their fears, confirm their suspicions, and help them throw rocks at their enemies."

Author Joe Vitale wrote: "Our goal as marketing and business people isn't to tell people what's wrong with them or to remind them of their pain, but to help them imagine and then experience the pleasure they long to have. It's noble, yes, and it works. Love moves everyone. Love is the great motivator. Love is the great pleasure trigger."

I'll add a few of my own. People want:

- To stop pain
- To feel good about themselves
- To feel appreciated and admired by others
- To feel powerful (some say that money and sex are part of this desire)
- To banish feelings of powerlessness
- To feel a spiritual connection
- To make a contribution—and to help others
- To be loved and to express their love—and feel connected to others

I invite you to find how your product or service fulfills the desires that I have noted above. Here's a secret: find something good, kind and wholesome that you help people with. This is the secret method to eliminate any hesitation you might have about marketing or selling. As I say with my clients: "Become a coach to action. A coach helps people do what they truly desire to do." Touch people's hearts and minds, and you'll get 'em to buy.

* * *

Now that we've covered what people really want and what motivates them to buy, it's time to brainstorm specific details about your product/service and start forming your marketing campaign.

9-Minute Method (#6): Circles and Triangle Process

Why You Need to Do This:

When preparing a marketing campaign, brainstorming is essential. It truly helps to use a process that gets your first ideas on paper quickly.

For many people, thoughts arise in a random order, so it helps to have areas on the paper that function as receptacles—almost like mail slots.

First, I'll show you the process, and then I'll demonstrate with my own example.

Step 1: Draw three circles.

Step 2: Label the circles:

a) Target Market

b) Where Target Market Is To Be Found; and

c) "What I naturally do well"

Step 3: Draw one triangle below the three circles (We call this the Triangle of Implementation.)

Step 4: In each of the three circles, quickly record ideas that are appropriate for the circle's label.

Step 5: In the triangle, write your first guesses about what you could do (implement) for your marketing activities (combining the above three elements).

Now, I'll share an example.

Circle #1: Target Market

Women business owners in business three years or longer*

Circle #2: Where Target Market Is to Be Found

Associations for women business owners

Circle #3: "What I naturally do well"

Speak to groups

Now it's time to take the above into account and *write something into the triangle that I can actually do.*

Triangle (combining the above three elements)

"Give a speech at a women's association meeting. During the speech, tell stories of how women business owners have saved money using methods that I teach."

* Why focus on women-owned businesses three years or older? This is about getting specific about the clientele you really want. People just starting their businesses are often scared and hesitant to spend money on training. This not an easy-to-sell-to population. On the other hand, people in business three years or longer have seen real-world ups and downs. They are more likely to want to take their business to a higher level, and they are more likely to invest in improving their situation than "wannabes" and novices.

The Exercise:

Now, it's your turn.

Step 1: Draw three circles.

Step 2: Label the circles:

a) Target Market

b) Where Target Market Is To Be Found; and

c) "What I naturally do well"

Step 3: Draw one triangle below the three circles (We call

this the Triangle of Implementation.)

Step 4: In each of the three circles, quickly record ideas that are appropriate for the circle's label.

Step 5: In the triangle, write your first guesses about what you could do (implement) for your marketing activities into the Triangle (combining the above three elements).

What was the purpose of the above exercise? You just had the opportunity to capture your first ideas. Then you were able to categorize them and build on those ideas. In the triangle you probably came up with some ideas of what to implement for your marketing campaign—not some vague goal such as "stir up more interest" but an actual, specific, doable task with a particular audience.

* * *

Sometimes a case study really cements an idea into place. You improve your marketing by setting up a system. Now Lois Creamer shares her system that a speaker can use for getting speaking engagements.

Productivity In Selling Speeches

by Lois Creamer

In order for this article to be most meaningful you need to read the previous post on speaking services. That post discussed how to approach, who to approach, what to say when you approach and more

(at http://bookmorebusiness.com/blog/2012/05/).

I'm going to share my qualifying system in this article. In order to be highly productive doing outbound selling either by phone, email or social media, you need to have some type of system that will tell you just how interested the prospect really is in you. I base mine on the three M's.

M = meeting. Do they have a specific meeting date? If they don't plans are still very uncertain.

M = money. This one is simple. Do they have enough to pay your fee?

M = motive. This means have they used someone like you in the past, or if not, do they seem interested in you and your information.

Pretty simple huh? The three M's. Here is the system to implement further.

If a prospect has 3 M's, they are the hottest of prospects! Highly interested. If you don't work with them on this specific program, odds are you will later. This is a level 1 lead.

If a prospect has 2 M's, this is still a high qualifier. Perhaps they have meeting and money but have yet to decide on motive or topic. This is a level 2 lead.

If a prospect has 1 M, it is a low level lead. Typically when qualifying someone here they have the one M of meeting. But they don't have any planned, so of course we aren't going to talk budget either. I also call level 3 leads "people who like to get stuff for free and suck the life out of your business."

I list the levels 1,2,3 in my ACT database (contact management system) under ID/Status. This allows you to pull out each as a group. Perhaps you want to send an email to levels 1 and 2 only. Easy!

Now this is productivity! Remember the levels are fluid. Perhaps a prospect is a level 1 lead but chooses someone else. Mark them down to a level 2 and proceed from there.

You should seek to "touch" each prospect who is a level 1 client once every 30-60 days.

When I say touch, I don't mean call! I only believe in calling a prospect when there is business to transact. By "touching" I mean keeping your name in front of the prospect. You can do this by emailing a newsletter, tip, sending an article, forwarding a new marketing piece or information about a new program, sending a testimonial or anything else that will make you "front of mind." Postcard marketing is still very effective! It is high touch, low tech, and if you do it, you will stand out.

If you do these things, you will really be running a speaking practice where we have prospects in the planning mode coming up at all times.

I hope you'll try my system. Let me know how it works for you!

Happy hunting!

Lois Creamer is both small business strategist and specialist! She speaks from experience! Her clients have adopted her philosophy of concept and outcome marketing and use of a positioning statement to successfully grow their businesses and increase profits. Her common sense ideas and high-energy approach make her a perfect choice for small business owners and entrepreneurs who want to learn new strategies that can be implemented immediately. Lois is the author of *Working Smart, Not Hard* as well as several audio programs.

Visit Lois at www.bookmorebusiness.com

* * *

Lois Creamer shared her system for gaining speaking engagements. Many small business owners find that they can increase their client base by giving speeches and sharing their expertise. It's a fast way to establish themselves as trustworthy and credible. Let's continue . . .

An important point about organizing a marketing campaign is to simply get started.

Many people get stuck because they cannot do something

perfectly. That is, their fear of appearing "imperfect" stops them from taking any action at all. Perfection has its place—like when a surgeon operated on one of my family members years ago. However, most things only need excellence. So . . . set your **own** criteria for excellence. How? Ask yourself these questions before you take action on a new marketing campaign:

1. What must be in this project?
2. What can be left out?
3. How long do you have to work on it?
4. What does the end user expect to find in this project?
5. How can you surprise and delight the customer?

These questions and your answers serve as a starting point for a strategic plan. Such a plan can help you *set criteria for excellence*.

Strategizing

by Linda L. Chappo

(an excerpt from *Full Strength Marketing: How You Can Use Your Hidden Strengths, Break Through Inner Barriers and Raise Your Profits*)

Strategizing benefits us in several ways by saving time, getting things done quickly and easily, and giving direction to our lives. Strategies help us to influence each other and the mass population. It's done everyday on the Internet, television and radio—and in books, magazines, newspapers. A strong marketer is more effective and accomplishes more by applying strategizing strengths to a marketing campaign.

Our next step is to delve into your process for creating a marketing strategy.

Three benefits of a marketing strategy are:

1. To unify your business's public and personal image

with your marketing materials, resulting in a balanced and magnetic public appeal.

2. To link a business with its target market.
3. To become a strong presence in your community and within your particular industry. It positions your business in front of your competition.

A strategy includes any marketing effort done more than once. Base your strategies on the relationship of three factors: position, niche and communication messages. Everything you do in your marketing campaign must attract the consumer, appeal to the person's sense of necessity, and create a sense of expectancy.

Many small business marketing campaigns are set up around events on the yearly calendar; consumers expect these social events to happen and look forward to the experience.

Plan a Calendar of Events

Before each new year begins, make it a priority to sit down with this book and figure out your marketing calendar of events. I suggest that you do this every November for the following year.

Do it before you get busy with the ever-hectic Thanksgiving and Christmas holiday seasons.

The best way to promote your small business for the year is to lay down the calendar in front of you, determine the busy times of the year, and mark those events for particular promotions. This gives you the ability to see when the slow times exist and plan specific promotions for those times as well.

The Five Advantages of Advance Planning

1. Prevents you from forgetting to do it during busy

times.

2. Provides a simple and direct timeline to follow.
3. Frees up your time to take care of details, meet with employees and get your customers excited about your projects. You'll feel a sense of satisfaction and readiness.
4. Helps you manage your time effectively and assures that each step in the process flows smoothly.
5. Gives ample time to correct any errors which might occur. Remember that nothing is written in stone, so if you unexpectedly hire a new employee with special strengths, or find a new product, you can always substitute one promotion for another if necessary.

The last thing you want to do is throw a promotion package together quickly at the last minute without much thought as to its content and effectiveness. Mistakes can occur, costing you both your money and your reputation. Mistakes can turn off your potential customer; she may think, "If the person is sloppy with an ad, then he'll be sloppy with my needs."

Also, make sure you devote the time to shop around for the best-priced media package.

When choosing which events to promote throughout the year, remember your vision or objective and your marketing strategy.

Events Calendar Process

The Events Calendar is a focal point of this system. Use the Events Calendar to pinpoint events that help you reach your primary objective for the year.

1. First write in all the holiday events that you will promote.

2. Add special events like your business's anniversary, any local fairs or festivities, or themed events.
3. List seasonal events such as proms, graduations, the wedding seasons and back-to-school.
4. Mark the obvious slow seasons for themed product or service promotions.

Maintain Balance

Create a balance in your calendar events schedule to allow your campaign to make consistent progress. You'll also need adequate time to rest, renew and resume. Resist the urge to do too many promotions all at once. It will confuse your employees and your

clients. A balanced schedule throughout the year is easier on your budget, too. Too much down time between promotions is also not helpful. Keep your messages consistent.

Choose Social Promotional Events

Here are ten possible promotional events:

1. Holiday events
2. Vacations
3. Community social events (festivals, fairs, parades, theater events, concerts, symphony or opera opening nights, and black tie affairs)
4. Personal rites of passage (weddings, graduations, proms, birthday parties, baptisms, religious confirmations, wedding and baby showers)
5. New products
6. New services
7. New employees
8. Your Grand Opening or Anniversary

9. Business renovations or change of location
10. When business needs a boost (an annual event specific to you)

Marketing experts recommend that you keep your business's name consistently in front of the public all year round.

Remember your primary objective. You'll be choosing important promotions that support your primary objective. Study this list of secrets to help you stay on course.

Six success secrets to event planning

Secret 1: Choose events that do the most for your business's image.

Participating in charity events, festivals, and parades are great for upgrading a business's image. There are other effective ways, depending on your location and your target market. For example, your upscale business will find a more lucrative market by promoting to area hotels during the summer or winter tourist season. Your budget-minded business will find more profit potential by marketing to a local college crowd during a Back-to-School sale. A designer clothing store would get more value out of a promotion directed towards convention attendees as opposed to a Country and Western Jamboree. Always remember the image you want to project.

Secret 2: Select events that help you to establish your position.

Choose a position strategy for your business (the first and most important strategy). Decide which events and promotions clarify your position and distinguish you as the market leader. For example, a speaker who guides people to get jobs could hold a "job-a-thon"—that is, she could coach twenty participants and see how many gain job interviews in one month. This process could help her gain a position as the Job Seeker's Coach.

Secret 3: Embrace events that attract your target market.

Tailor your promotions to your target market, which will desire and purchase your products and services. If your target market consists mainly of senior citizens, then avoid advertising your services related to the prom, wedding services, or back-to-school seasons. Local health fairs or a Seniors' Center would be better. You might trade Appreciation Certificates with businesses that seniors frequent: doctors, health clinics, cafes or coffee shops, health food stores and others. Focus on clothing or department stores that appeal to seniors.

Secret 4: Determine which media will support your purpose for each event, and your primary objective for the year.

Inexpensive flyers and coupons will work fine for many events. Sometimes newspapers and radio will do the best job. Perhaps direct mail would be most effective in establishing the intimate contact you need. When I owned my salon business, local newspapers would offer special advertising rates to all merchants who participated in an event. Our Merchants' Association would buy a half page or full page advertisement at a better than usual rate. Invite other local merchants to join you in buying advertising space and save money for everyone.

Secret 5: Decide which events/media will be within your budget.

No doubt about it, experience helps you effectively gauge

the right budget and which media to choose for promotions. Your decisions will depend upon the extent of exposure you want and which media reaches your target audience. If flyers and coupons reach your target market most effectively, that is the media to use. If your experience demonstrates that the Internet or direct mail works best, then stay with that medium. Here's the important point: if a more expensive medium or event brings in the business you want, then it's worth investing with it for that promotion. The money will return to you. Don't bother wasting less money on an affordable promotion that does nothing for your business.

Secret 6: Network your way to success.

Network and ask other business owners about their experience with printers, copy shops and direct mail companies. Cost, reliability, quality and results are what counts. Ask about their experience with different social events. Find out which media they used and the response rate. (Also, consider doing some form of "joint venture" or teaming up to target similar clientele.)

Action Steps

1. How will you maintain balance in your marketing plan?

2. Which events will you choose for your campaign?

Remember that in the beginning, your promotions may be subject to trial and error. However, your groundwork here will help you to plan your future promotions and advertising more effectively.

Develop Your Media Plan

For every promotion, you'll need a media plan that includes how and where to promote your business. Add this information to your calendar of events.

Read the following information to discover which media will best reach your target market, stay within your budget, and allow you to reach your primary objective this year. There are four areas to develop: public relations, print, broadcast and digital media.

Public relations

Public relations is about keeping the public informed and interested in your business. It encompasses all the activities you do to obtain free exposure for your business. Some examples of public relations are announcements, press releases, feature stories, interviews, press kits and press conferences.

Local newspapers and radio stations are often open to interviews and feature stories, usually as personal interest stories. Send a light, human-interest story to the features editor of your newspaper. Remember to clip articles that feature your business. Save them for press kits and portfolios about your business.

Print media

This area contains all printed materials via ink on paper—including newspapers, telephone books (*The Yellow Pages*), flyers, business cards, and brochures.

Advertising

Advertising attracts attention to the small or home-based business and creates the most favorable impression on the public. This in turn expands the growth and development of your business. It is a sales proposition in which you are getting the consumer's attention to mentally involve them with the product or service. Print pertains to flyers, coupons, door hangers, and anything not included in other advertising.

Direct mail advertising

Direct mail coupons and introductory letters are an effective advertising tool to get new business. A 1-5% return is considered good. There are two benefits of using direct mail: its accountability and how quickly you know the results of your investment. Remember, even if you don't receive the response you expect from the first mailing, your business's name and service is still getting the most effective exposure available.

The way to achieve success in direct mail is to make the right offer, to the right prospect, at the right time, and in the right way. You must present your information in a visually attractive manner, and remember to make the offer irresistible. You must also create a consistent message and look.

Direct mail is highly effective because it creates a more intimate contact with the reader. With a direct mail campaign, you directly interact with potential customers in a personal way. Your letter or coupon goes directly into their home with their name and address on the envelope. Direct mail includes letters of introduction, newsletters, direct mail coupons and more.

Get a clear idea of a market that would find your products and services valuable. A demographic survey, which allows you to pinpoint who your potential customers are, will increase your chances of success.

"Testing" with direct mail is vital. Try several differently worded introductory letters, mail them to your target market and observe which letter creates the most responses. Start with your own customer mailing list: a) begin with your customer card files for current names, b) use names from previous contests or drawings, and c) ask current customers for names of friends and relatives (a referral list). Here's an idea: give a small gift in return for five or ten referrals. Now would be a good time to leave a customer mailing list form at your front desk.

Two crucial points in direct mail: a) it is better to send fewer letters to a well-targeted list of 300 than to send to a "random" list of 3,000 and b) to raise your response level to 17% (as noted by researchers who track this process) use up to four repeat mailings per prospective client.

Magazine and newspaper advertising

Recent years have seen the disappearance of numerous magazines and newspapers. Magazines are generally a poor choice for a small or home-based business advertisement. It's just too costly. A magazine's territory is too wide to benefit most small businesses. You will pay high exposure rates for consumers who live too far away.

However, if your business lends itself to magazine advertisements (a mail-order firm for example), the most effective number of placements is a minimum of five pages per year.

You may fare better with regional magazines or those that are directed toward specific industries: insurance, real estate, medical, or hospitality.

Yellow Pages advertising

Classified ads in the Yellow Pages provide a certain amount of exposure. Yellow Pages advertisements don't necessarily motivate people to buy from you or frequent your business. Once you have already motivated them with other media, the Yellow Pages pull them in. (In this time of Internet searches, many claim Yellow Pages lack the impact of earlier years.)

The advantages of this media are that you have constant exposure, everyday, for 24 hours a day. Yellow Pages are most effective for businesses whose name begins with the letter A. Remember that every business and home has a phone book. However, recognize these three disadvantages to the yellow pages. You can't update your advertisement whenever you feel the need; restrictions require that you make changes at one particular time of the year when the telephone book is due for republishing. This may happen a year from when you need it, so you must plan accordingly. Secondly, a large ad can be quite expensive. You may or may not be able to recoup your costs. Thirdly, nowadays, people tend to rely more on the Internet for their search efforts.

Broadcast media—radio and television

Radio and television can help to supplement your advertising campaign by reaching a wider audience. Radio is less expensive and it also gives wide exposure. You will reach a broader range of consumers than through the newspaper or other media. Radio is everywhere: in our cars, our homes, in stores, on the streets, and on our headsets. There are many varieties of stations from which to choose: all-news, all-sports, top 40 music, classical, country, jazz, ethnic, and more.

There is a limitation of two minutes or less for radio spots, so you must make the sale in that time constraint. You must present a problem and demonstrate why your product or service can provide the solution. Make sure to state the price and possibly a money-back guarantee. Create a sense of urgency or a reason to act "now." It's helpful to use a phone number that is easy to remember. I recall that the authors of the *Chicken Soup for the Soul* Series used the phone number: 1-800-SOUP-BOOK.

The principles of radio advertising are:

1. Talk one-to-one with the listener (talk about benefits).
2. Focus on one idea, creatively expressed to get attention.
3. Stretch the listener's imagination by creating atmosphere.
4. Be topical by sending messages relative to the season (Christmas, Valentine's Day, Mother's Day).
5. Measure the response by asking new customers if they heard your radio announcement.

I used radio advertising a couple of times with only moderate success. I advertised in conjunction with a co-op agreement. The script was good and professional; however, consistent use is necessary to get a great response.

A program host at the station can read your radio advertisement or commercial. Listen at the time your announcement is getting airplay to hear how it sounds. Record it if possible. Remember that people are listening in their cars, not necessarily through a high-tech stereo system. Having an announcer read your script live has drawbacks because he or she may have a bad day or read it too fast.

You can do pre-recorded messages yourself if you have a pleasing voice. Pre-recorded announcements in a voice that appeals to you will always sound the same and be delivered in a style that expresses your professionalism. Reading from a script will prevent errors, but practice enough to sound natural. Music evokes feelings and emotions without pictures.

Other than advertising, you can use talk and information shows as a vehicle to promote your business. Find a local station where the host interviews guest speakers. Talk about a specialty area where you are an expert.

Television requires a lot of money to buy advertising space. You must be strong at creating an attention-getting advertisement. You have only three seconds to grab the consumer's attention. Business owners find that hiring professional consultants or ad agencies may be necessary to gain the expertise needed.

Digital media

The Internet—online marketing

Your online presence is like having a marketing staff working for you 24/7. On your website, you can share your newsletters or offer customer education programs and sell your products in a catalog format. You can accept orders online, by fax or telephone. People are interested in websites that have up-to-date, interesting content. They also like interactive sites that are easy to navigate. Websites must be constantly updated and improved; otherwise, people will be bored and won't return. My co-author Tom Marcoux provides free material at his blog

BeHeardandBeTrusted.com (with a new article every week). He gains subscribers to his free enewsletter "Success Secrets." Occasionally, he holds a special promotion around Valentine's Day and the Holiday Season that he promotes through his email list. Repeatedly, he gets immediate orders because he provides two details: (1) a deadline and (2) an enticing free offer (like an exclusive downloadable audio program).

Another way to increase traffic on your website is to

subscribe to a service such as Yahoo Directory. Such subscriptions improve your ranking in search results so potential customers get to your site sooner, and your company description will be written by a professional search director (that is, a person, not a machine). A number of website owners use Google Ads to bring potential customers to their websites.

My co-author Tom Marcoux writes a blog at www.BeHeardandBeTrusted.com. He reports that his articles are often shared on Facebook, Twitter and Linkedin.com.

Be careful about what you place on the Internet. Consider submitting your blog entries to a team member or friend for comments before you publish your thoughts. Your associate could save you from needless embarrassment. My co-author Tom Marcoux says, "A blog and email are like cockroaches; they never go away. I am careful to have a team member look at my broadcast messages to my e-subscribers because once the message is sent, I can't take it back."

Promotion Reminders

Plan each promotion from beginning to end, and review it periodically to implement improvements.

Make Final Decisions

1. Make the final decisions of events to promote.
2. Determine your budget allowance for each promotion.
3. Develop a theme and give it a tagline.
4. If needed, determine which products to order for the promotion, either pre-packaged items or additional stock.
5. Determine the suitable media or combination of media to use: Internet, billboard, radio, print, cable TV or other.

6. If using print media, decide which elements to use: coupons, direct mail, newspaper, flyers, postcards or other. Find out the cost of each.
7. Write your promotional pieces and target them to a specific audience.
8. When necessary, contact your graphic designer, advertising agency or printer to determine required lead time for printed pieces. Your local copy center is also a good source for short, uncomplicated photocopying.
9. Determine when to send out mailings, remembering that mail service is sometimes slow during the holiday seasons.
10. Remember to notify your employees of all promotions far enough in advance so they can verbally interact with clients. Train employees to use new services or product lines so they can speak from experience.
11. Increase your effectiveness by telephone follow-up calls.
12. Coordinate your social media marketing efforts with Twitter, Facebook, LinkedIn and your own blog.

List Exact Media Details for Each Promotion

1. Names and phone numbers of newspapers, radio stations, direct mail companies, cable TV, billboard sign companies and others.
2. Free publicity opportunities.
3. Costs of printed or photocopied materials.
4. Dates and sizes of ads.
5. Frequency of advertising.

Do a Product and Equipment Analysis

Begin with a description and cost for products: For each

promotion, note which products to order and the expected costs.

Inside display: Acquire point-of-purchase displays for various promotions. Manufacturers provide displays that professionally showcase new products, novelty items or anything that applies to your retail business.

Equipment: Various promotions may require the purchase of additional equipment. New gimmicks and gadgets are available every year.

Include a Marketing Budget:

Total marketing budget . . . . $__

Budget for each promotion . . . . . $__

Budget for new products . . . . $__

Budget for new equipment . . . . . $__

Linda L. Chappo became a marketing specialist to enhance her first business which did so well that she sold it and traveled the world. She then earned degrees in graphic arts and culinary arts. Her current businesses relate to those fields, to spirituality, and to coaching small business owners. Linda helps small business owners overcome fears that may keep them from reaching their full potential. Her focus is on how small business owners already have everything they need within them, for successful marketing and for a successful life. Linda is also the author of *Marry Your Self First: Your Key to Manifesting Loving Relationships* and is the founder of both HearttoHeartLiving.com and

WeighLessExpress.com. She authored *How to Organize Your Marketing Campaign* and *How to Make it Big in the Hair Salon Business*. Reach her through HearttoHeartLiving.com and WeighLessExpress.com

* * *

Now the material in Linda L. Chappo's book excerpt may seem daunting. I find that setting up a list and breaking the process into small steps that you work on daily (perhaps, 20 minutes) makes the process feasible and less intimidating. Now John S. Rhodes will share 35 questions that can help you strategically plan your Product Launch. You'll notice that he begins with a story. Often, marketers use a story to seize the attention of the reader.

Product Launch Checklist
by John S. Rhodes

I'm going to give you a very simple **product launch checklist** that I've used with enormous success. It's AWESOME. And, it's a gift. Nothing for sale here, OK?

But, before I spill the beans… I want to tell you about my first experience with **Jeff Walker.**

It was 4 years ago. Jeff was promoting Product Launch Formula and I was watching it all very closely. I almost bought the product… but decided not to pull the trigger.

I was afraid. I was scared. "Too much money…!" went through my brain again and again. (Fear is the mind killer!)

The truth is that I definitely had enough money **but I just didn't have the courage to make the investment.** I let fear kick my ass.

So, I missed the offer. But then… Jeff re-opened the cart!

OK, so my initial reaction was ***"Yippee! I really am ready to INVEST NOW!"*** but my logical brain triggered some ANGER. You see, I felt like Jeff pulled a quick one… I thought the offer was actually closed. It was bologna that it was opening again.

I thought: **FALSE SCARCITY.**

At first, I was going to let it go… but then, I'm like… this is unfair. This is crap!

So, I wrote a note to Jeff. I wrote 5-6 very long paragraphs about how I wanted to invest in Product Launch Formula but that I didn't pull the trigger and missed the deadline, but that I was very disappointed with the false scarcity. (I was steaming mad by the end!)

I knew that Jeff would NEVER write back. "This multi-million dollar guru will NOT write me back..." But, at least I felt better, right?

Then, something shocking happened. Seriously, this blew my socks right off.

JEFF WALKER WROTE ME BACK.

It was not some lame boilerplate response... it wasn't just a few words... it wasn't just 1-2 sentences. Jeff wrote back a very long, logical and clear response to every single thing I brought up. Quite literally, my jaw dropped.

I won't go into all the details but I will tell you two important things:

1. **There was no "false scarcity" at all.** There were some refunds and credit card declines so there was room in the PLF training program. This was a good reason for the cart re-open and it was totally, 100% ethical. Sure, it gave Jeff a reason to make more money, but it was not a "fake" re-open just to extract more cash. It's bigger and more strategic than that. (There's a big mini-lesson here for anyone paying attention to this strategy; huge value here!)

2. **I bought Product Launch Formula** after reading Jeff's long, from-the-heart note to me. The investment still made me a little nervous because it was the biggest money I ever spent online. However, I can honestly say that **Jeff's PLF training program has helped me more than any other marketing training program... EVER.** Yes, that includes

great content from folks like Gary Halbert, Dan Kennedy, Frank Kern and others. I can't give a perfect estimate, but I know that it's responsible for **over $100,000 in additional sales in my business...** probably much more.

And, here's something else...

In 2010 I did a bunch of work for Jeff Walker behind the scenes. I can't go into the details out of respect for Jeff's business and because of a non-disclosure agreement (NDA) that I signed. But, I was behind-the-scenes for more than 8 months and it was an amazing experience... mostly because **Jeff is the "real deal" ... down-to-Earth, sincere and absolutely focused on customer success.**

OK, so I'm telling you this because it's a story you cannot hear from anyone else... it's my story about Jeff. But, now YOU understand my experience and you know that Product Launch Formula is amazing... and that Jeff can transform your life. **He's a class act.**

But, enough about me –!

Now, let's talk about how I can help you with my **Product Launch Checklist.**

Big Fat Disclaimer: This is about reducing mistakes, not transforming chicken poop into gold eagle coins. :)

Here we go:

* **What's the goal for your launch?** What do you expect? Specifically: when your launch is over how much money do you expect, how much will your list grow, and what do you want? Write these goals down before your launch. Be specific. Be able to measure your success.

* **What's your timeline for the prelaunch, launch and post launch?** What are the dates of the launch content being distributed? When does the cart go live? When do you reach out to your list? When do you reach out to JVs and affiliates,

if you're doing a big launch? Again, be very specific. Get a calendar out and write down the dates, with actions required and who is responsible, if you have a team.

* **Who is your ideal customer?** As Eben Pagan and Jeff Walker would ask: Who is your avatar? Specifically: Write out a clear description of your customer in terms of annual income, age, gender, habits, hobbies, appearance, and more. Have this person clear in your mind. If your "avatar" was sitting at your kitchen table… what would they look like and what would you say? What words and phrases matter? What would get them excited? What keeps them up at night?

* **What is your main hook?** What is your core offer? Be specific about the hook… what is the one thing that will grab attention and keep your prospects engaged, thrilled and otherwise mesmerized? Be specific about the offer… what are you going to be selling? What is the content? What is the format? What is delivery timeline? What is the name of the product? What are the bonuses?

Wow… right?

There are no less than 35 questions above! Simply take those questions… and start answering them. Start to dig into this Product Launch Checklist.

Then, launch! Enjoy the money, list building and expert status. Explode in your market. Get the power and respect you deserve.

OK, here's what you need to do next… to burn this into your brain… take action!

John S. Rhodes is an entrepreneur, best-selling author of *Money Leaves Clues,* husband and father. His clients include tens of thousands of small business owners but also Fortune 500 corporations such as IBM and Lockheed Martin. John has mentored and coached many of the most successful online and direct marketers in the world. www.JohnSRhodes.com

* * *

Remember, marketing is a process. Start small. Do a little each day (like making a plan for your next marketing campaign) and you'll reap the rewards.

Points to Remember:

*** Secret #6: People procrastinate because they don't know how to do marketing.**

*** Your Countermeasure:**
Focus on two important elements of marketing. Identify some small steps you can do. Perhaps you'll write five rough draft headlines for a press release today. Take action with what you know. And then add perhaps 20 minutes of reading each day. Soon you'll know more about marketing than many other small business owners. Make incremental progress.

* * * * * *

Secret #7: People procrastinate because they anticipate pain.

Say "marketing" to a number of small business owners, and they'll say, "I'd rather do anything else! Run 20 miles. Filing in the office. And I hate filing!" So what do many of us do about something that will cause pain? We avoid it. As a number of biologists will say, "The organism protects itself from pain."

You want success and prosperity—yes? What will that take? Overcoming procrastination and doing marketing activities. Let's get started . . .

When Marketing Doesn't Feel Good to You

Have you ever said to a friend: "I don't like marketing or selling"? I hear you.

This is a major opportunity to reframe the whole situation. I have worked with a number of clients and helped them transform the idea of "marketing" into being a "coach to action."

What does a good coach do?

"She helps you get done what you know you need to do," said my client Mirna. Yes! And whose agenda is it? "The person getting the coaching," Mirna concluded.

So to accomplish this empowering reframing of the whole strong marketing process, ask yourself these questions (and write down your answers in a personal journal—or better yet—your Marketing Plan binder):

1. What do you like about your work?
2. What's the best part of your work?
3. How do you help people?
4. When you're feeling good about your work, what is going on?

(Question 3 is part of the process of positioning your business.)

Now from this framework, imagine that you're going to help people get the advantages of working with you. The new clients are going to greatly benefit from interacting with you. And if they are not a match, you're going to help them in some way (refer them to someone who can help, or send a helpful link to an article).

This leads to an empowering phrase: "It's all good."

Now, we can approach marketing as a benevolent process.

It's all good. That's better!

* * *

If you're anticipating pain related to marketing activities, become strategic in how you build up a reserve of energy.

Gain Energy so You Do the Rough Parts of Marketing

Imagine that you need to write some material ("copy") for a new website—and you're really not in the mood!

Here are three methods to get going:

Call a friend

You can say: "Is this an okay time to talk? (she says 'yes') I've got to write something for a website. Can I throw a couple of ideas around for 2 minutes with you?" Then you start talking about the material. You can take notes, or some of my clients prefer to record their side of the conversation.

Draw "balloons"

Draw five balloons and then place ideas in them. You will draw lines to connect them later. For example, you could write: "how to overcome procrastination"; "pain"; "help"; "solution"; and "relief." You can also number the ideas in order of importance. You might come up with a headline like: "Would you like to stop procrastination from causing you pain?"

Ask, "Where is the joy?"

So many times we get caught up in the pain of the moment—or avoiding imagined pain. Instead, target what good feelings your effective marketing efforts will create.

For example, some of us enjoy getting a "thank you" email for a job well done. Or an author may relish signing books and shaking hands with happy workshop attendees. Ask yourself: "Where is the joy?" And then you may discover a spark of renewed energy.

Marketing is accomplished by placing one foot in front of the other. Just take the next step.

* * *

9-Minute Method (#7): Transform "Work Hard" to "Work Joy"

Why You Need to Do This:

If marketing is just "working hard" to you, you may put it off. And that will torpedo your business. You need to overcome that avoidance, and here we'll talk about how to do just that.

Secondly, stop bragging about "working hard." Why? Because it saps your energy. Instead, find where the joy is or can be in your work. Instead of "work hard," look for the "work joy." What does that mean? It means that *you can do something* to make work a more pleasant experience. And this will help with your marketing. How? Like anything else, marketing takes energy and focus. You need to protect your personal energy.

Bragging about "working hard" is just as ineffective as complaining in these ways:

- "I *have to* do marketing calls. I hate cold calling."
- "I *have to* write an enewsletter. I'm a lousy writer. It takes forever."

I'll share a personal example. In the past, I'd do just about anything before writing the crucial description paragraph for my new book at Amazon.com. Why? It's intimidating.

The description must be concise, precise, and compelling. Then, I learned to transform the onerous task of perfecting a description paragraph into something of "work joy." How? I changed the wording of my thoughts from "Damn! I ***have to*** write a description paragraph" into "I ***get to*** write a quick rough draft. No worries. Just toss some words on the page. And then I ***get to*** work with David and Johanna on the revision." This works for me because I feel more energy when I collaborate with team members.

Saying to myself "Once I write the first draft, I get to work with David and Johanna on the revision" perked me right up! Why? Because I enjoy going over things with my editors. Listening to them, finding ways to incorporate their suggestions, finding just the right way to reword things—this feels fun to me!

Words can serve as triggers that move your mood in a certain direction. Look at these "have to" phrases:

- I have to make cold calls.
- I have to write an enewsletter.
- I have to write the copy for a new ad.

"Have to" is a trigger to feel down and, perhaps, frustrated.

Instead, use "I get to." I'll give you another real example. During a semester, there are multiple times when I must grade 120 papers by college and graduate students. I used to say, "I *have to* grade the papers." Boom! Energy gone, my shoulders drooped, and I felt so tired.

Things turned around when I began saying, "I *get to* grade the papers. That is, I get to *encourage* the students with my comments on their papers."

The Exercise:

Pull out a sheet of paper and draw two columns. Label

Column #1 as "I Have to." Designate Column #2 as "I Get to"

Here are examples:

I Have to:

I have to make cold calls <becomes>

I Get to:

I ***get to*** make warm calls. I'll call people who are in the same LinkedIn Group that I'm in. I'll find their phone numbers on their websites. When I call, I ***get to*** feel excited about the service I provide and share that with people.

Now, it's your turn. Take five of your usual "I have to..." comments and transform them into "I get to . . ." statements.

At first glance, the phrase "I get to" may seem simplistic. Worse, it may feel ineffective, even naïve. As with much in life, you don't know if it works for you until you try it. Experience shows that it works, though. Why? Our brain responds to a stimulus. "I have to" is a downer stimulus. However, "I get to" is an *energizing* stimulus. And pause for a moment. How can you transform the situation into an "I get to" opportunity?

For example, I once needed to prepare before sitting down with my employer so that I could ask for a raise. I transformed my preparation with these phrases: "I get to ask my friends for support. I get to rehearse with them before the important meeting. ***I get to feel their support***."

Another way to energize yourself is to ask a question. "Why are marketing calls an 'I get to' opportunity for me?" Maybe answering that question will spark an idea so that you can change your approach to making such phone calls.

Personally I've found saying "I get to" increases my own energy.

* * *

Many successful people I have interviewed have said that they gain energy by *skillfully* setting goals. The right goal gives them inspiration. Now Beth Barany shares her system of goal setting.

Overcome Writers Block: Setting Goals, Writing to Win

By Beth Barany

(Adapted and Excerpted from her best-selling book, *Overcome Writer's Block: 10 Writing Sparks to Jumpstart Your Creativity*.)

Spark Two: Write to Goal: Write to Win. Write and Finish that Book! : 10-5-1 Goal Setting

You have it. Drive. Motivation. Inspiration.

All great success comes with a plan, a structured series of action steps. It takes movement and an outpouring of energy. Action makes dreams and visions manifest. It's a beautiful and powerful thing to see one's dreams and visions in tangible, touch-me real form, whether you want to write plays, poems, novels, short stories, screenplays, or nonfiction.

You have it. Drive, motivation, inspiration, but just not today. Today you don't remember why you want to write that novel, screenplay, memoir or expert nonfiction book. Because when you sit down to write, your mind goes blank, or worse yet, the story is mapped out, but there's no juice. *There's no there there.* (As an Oakland resident, I'm entitled to use this. Attributed to Gertrude Stein.)

What to do? Oh, the travails of a writer!

Never fear, goal setting is here. Now before you moan and groan that goal setting is for sissies, I mean, business types, remember that your big, unwieldy book or project is well, big, and needs planning to succeed. Like a house needs an architectural drawing, or a football team needs a game plan. Whether we like it or not, planning is a very important part of any big endeavor. So yes, that means all of us writers.

Yes, us writers. And while we're at it, if we're going to plan a novel or screenplay or a nonfiction book on our expertise, why wouldn't we also plan our career or plan the whole arc of the writing project? And to clear up any confusion, you can use planning to plot, or brainstorm scenes, even if you are plot-averse, a "pantser." (Pantser = seat-of-the-pants writer, as opposed to a "plotter," someone who plots.)

Be in Charge of Your Writing Plan

Being in charge means finding a way to plan that works for you. I've found a fun planning tool that works well for me. I suggest using it once to see if you like it, then implement it every week or every month, as a way to stay in touch with your next action items. I dubbed it the 10-5-1 and learned this technique from leadership trainer and friend, Greg Norte, owner and founder of Armada Training Solutions. The 10-5-1 technique is about thinking big on the one hand, and about creating manageable structure, on the other. The end result? The 10-5-1 will help you develop a strong plan of action.

Make sure to make your goals SMART.

SMART goals applies to a common and useful business acronym and represents a goal-setting tool, explained below. Taken from a forthcoming book, *The Eight Steps to Successful*

Entrepreneurship, by one of my clients, Fred Bauer of Abundance Business Coaching, I've adapted it to fit writers.

Specific – Be very specific about your goal or goals. You could say, "Write a book," or you could be more specific and say, "I'm going to write a long comedic fantasy novel that's a cross between Douglas Adams and Patrick O'Brien."

Measurable – Make sure you can measure your goal so you know when you have achieved it. This could be counting your words, pages, or your time, or some combination of the three.

Achievable – State your goal in the present or past tense as if you have already achieved it, making especially sure the goal is achievable. Is it realistic for you to expect you can write your novel in three months? Maybe, if you're an experienced fiction writer and you've already done that. More achievable for a first time novelist may be one year, or it may be five, as it was for me.

Results-oriented – Will the work you do lead to results that you value? Finishing a book, writing a book, outlining a book are all steps that lead to the result of having written a book.

Time – Have a specific date for when your goal will be achieved. Give your project a deadline that you can mark on the calendar and celebrate its completion, or course correct when that date is reached.

A Note on Course Correction

A nautical term, course correction refers to the need to make adjustments on the way to a destination. One angle of approach may not work so you may need to change it, all the while not letting go of the final goal.

Now to the 10-5-1 process…

The Power of Ten

Start with thinking where you want to be with your writing and writing career in ten-years. Write down the date exactly ten years from now. List everything, your wildest dreams, your just-for-you dreams. Dream big, dream outrageous and true to you. This is about what you really want, no matter how outlandish, no matter what anyone else might think. Reach for the stars and you may just hit the moon. Be glorious, rich and full in your vision. I dare you to make it bold. Take the time to answer this question in full. Your writing vision can be one thing or many things. Declare your dream in the present tense or by stating, "In ten years, by [state the date], I have ..."

By declaring our dreams, we may wonder: "Will I be letting myself down? What if I don't reach my goal?" Well, it won't be for a lack of trying. And remember, our big dreams are not created in a vacuum; they involve many others and so are, to a certain extent, beyond our control. That's okay. Let's focus on what we can control. And that is the writing.

My ten-year goal: By **September 14, 2017**, I am a New York Times best-selling writer in fiction and nonfiction; I have produced several films; I continue to generate fun, exciting and useful creative material whether in print, online or other mediums, not yet invented.

Now it's your turn to write down your ten-year goal or goals, pertaining to your creativity. Fill out the bonus worksheet, write in your notebook, or use your computer. No excuses. Because your dreams start today. Right now. Right here and now. Congratulations for taking the first step and writing your dreams down.

The Power of Five

Now that you know your ten-year goal, let's look at the

five-year goal. Fill out the bonus worksheet, write in your notebook, or use your computer. Where do you need to be in five years to make your ten-year goals a reality? For the purposes of this article I'll pick one of my ten-year goals, not all. You can do this exercise for all of them if you want.

In five years, by **September 14, 2012**, I will have written and completed two more books in my fantasy series, found a publisher, secured an agent, and have the series published.

Now it's your turn to write down your five-year goal or goals, pertaining to your creativity. Fill out the bonus worksheet, write in your notebook, or use your computer. Congratulations for taking the second step and writing your dreams down.

In One Year…

Let's come closer to home, and look at our one-year goal. Where will you be in one year to help you accomplish your five-year goal? Make this goal doable, and as stated above, make this goal SMART.

One-year goal: By **Sept. 14, 2008**, I will have completed editing Book II in the series and will have started on Book III.

Now it's your turn to write down your one-year goal or goals, pertaining to your creativity. Fill out the bonus worksheet, write in your notebook, or use your computer. Congratulations for taking the third step and writing your dreams down.

In Just Six Months…

Taking it even closer, let's look at six months. Notice if you have any anxiety or excitement about setting a six-month goal for yourself. Anxiety and excitement are two sides of the same coin, so it's good to notice where you are on the spectrum. And if you are bored with your goal at this point, it's good to notice that too, and see if you picked a goal that truly you care about, or maybe you picked a ten-year goal that your mind thinks you should pick, that may not be yours truly, and instead may be someone else's. If so, take a look at whose goal it is. Or, you may have picked a ten-year goal that is really a five-year goal. If that's the case, move the ten-year goal into the five-year slot, and choose something more daring as your ten-year goal.

At the six-month mark, what do you need to do to make your one-year goal a reality?

Six months: By **March 14, 2008**, I have finished the first draft of Book II, and am getting ready to start the editing process.

Now it's your turn to write down your six-month goal or goals, pertaining to your creativity. Fill out the bonus worksheet, write in your notebook, or use your computer. Congratulations for taking the fourth step and writing your dreams down.

In Only One Month!

One month: ah, now this is where you start looking at what you can accomplish short term. Don't forget to make it SMART. What do you need to do this month to make your six-month goal a reality?

One month/Four calendar weeks: By **October 12, 2007**, I will have written four more chapters on my book, completing the first draft through Chapter 20.

Now it's your turn to write down your one-month goal or goals, pertaining to your creativity. Fill out the bonus worksheet, write in your notebook, or use your computer. Congratulations for taking the fourth step and writing your dreams down.

One Week from Today

Now we get to the nitty-gritty, things that you can write in your calendar. There's not a whole lot to explain. Just be sure that the activities you choose to accomplish in a week support your one-month goal and are SMART.

One week: By **September 21, 2007**, I will have written and completed Chapter 18, and will be halfway through Chapter 19.

Now it's your turn to write down your one-week goal or goals, pertaining to your creativity. Fill out the bonus worksheet, write in your notebook, or use your computer. Congratulations for taking the fifth step and writing your dreams down.

Today/Tomorrow

What will you do today or tomorrow that makes your one-week goal a reality?

Today/Tomorrow: By **Sept. 15, 2007**, I will have completed Chapter 17, and started Chapter 18.

Now it's your turn to write down your today/tomorrow goal or goals, pertaining to your creativity. Fill out the bonus worksheet, write in your notebook, or use your computer. Congratulations for taking the sixth step and writing your dreams down.

A Plan that Comes with Teeth

So there you have it. An action plan. So now what? Revisit your 10-5-1 every week or month. Generally, I revisit it Sundays with my husband. We both take a leisurely breakfast and sit together on the patio to plan our one week and today/tomorrow goals. When we hit the one-month mark, we revise them too. When I hit March 2008 I will set new six-month writing goals.

Let me know how it goes.

Happy goal setting!

***

PS. It's 2012, and while things haven't happened exactly as planned, I do have two books done in my fantasy series, the second one due out this fall.

You can buy all 10 Sparks in *Overcome Writer's Block: 10 Writing Sparks to Jumpstart Your Creativity* on the Kindle, Smashwords, and now, AtContent, where bloggers and readers can help spread the word and sell the book.

Bestselling Author's Coach, **Beth Barany**, www.bethbarany.com/ is dedicated to the notion that all is better with play. An author too, she's the author of the 2011 award-winning young adult fantasy novel *Henrietta The Dragon Slayer*, http://author.bethbarany.com/ as well as of the bestselling nonfiction books for authors and aspiring authors, www.amazon.com/Writers-Adventure-Guide-Stages-Writing/dp/0982344252

Beth gives away 10 spots per month for a 30-Minute Complimentary Coaching Session. ***First Come First Serve!*** Schedule yours today! Click now to schedule yours: Beth's Online Scheduler, https://my.timedriver.com/67RH1

* * *

Many small business owners set a goal for a number of marketing calls per day. But still a number of them procrastinate. Why? Many do not feel good about how they make such calls. Now, Jeanna Gabellini shares how to empower your selling efforts.

THE Sales Conversation for People Who Hate Selling

by Jeanna Gabellini

It's easy to tell someone about your product or service

when they casually ask. But the most well-spoken people fumble when it comes time to ask for the sale. It's almost universally an internal, "Ewwwwww." Then, after the fact, you think of all the cooler things you could've said.

Unless you LOVE sales, asking for the business can be awkward.

Let me take away your discomfort. We can also take away all the word-for-word responses to your potential customer's objections. And for Pete's sake, stop going in for the kill in your written marketing.

It's all about truth. Your truth. And what you see is true for your potential customers.

Here's the best way to make the sale with grace.

You must always be looking through the lens of your customer's eyes.

They are looking for your product or service because of WHAT pain, desire or problem?

What's their next logical step?

- What would prevent them from saying YES?
- What would make it easy for them to say YES?

Keep those answers in mind when you speak to them, verbally or when marketing. And guide them, like they were your friend, to the solution.

For example, when I have a conversation on the phone with someone who needs my services, I ask them several questions to zero in on the "real" problem or desire. That way I can cut through all their B.S. when I'm coaching them to the next step.

I ask myself, are they the right fit for my company? If yes, I think about which services would help them short-term and long-term. Then I offer them up and tell them why I think each would serve them. I ask them if they have questions or concerns.

I am absolutely not attached to their answer, no matter how much I need the money.

I stay in service mode. In service of them. I want them to get their ideal solution, even if that means referring them to something outside of my company.

Connect to your heart. This makes it easy to say what you truly feel is their next step in the solution process.

Some people can't deal with long-term solutions because they're so focused on getting a cheap quick-fix now. Others just want the pain to go away ASAP and they just grab for anything immediate so they can move on. They don't give a rip about the future, they only see their now. I then give them my spiel about how making a choice based on a quick fix will end up costing them more energy, time, and money.

It's true.

If you feel this person isn't your ideal client, or you know they'll return the product, tell them they would be better served by doing A, B or C. Don't offer them your services if you don't really feel juiced about it.

When you're writing copy for your webpage or marketing, act like you are writing to ONE person. A person that you love engaging with and who has everything you want in a customer. Act like they came to you for the exact issue or dream that you love solving or creating.

You don't have to "pitch" or try hard to get the sale. You are still guiding them to their next step. You'll throw in some education, too. People who are not educated make poor buying decisions.

Truth.

Heart.

Get inside your ideal customer's head.

Listen for the real problem or desire.

Educate.

Guide them to the next step.

Make saying YES easy, comfortable and exciting!

Whether you thank them in person, by phone, email auto responder or thank you page on your website…you want them to feel like they just made the best choice ever! And they did if you followed the steps above.

Never use someone else's script for selling if it doesn't feel like a fuzzy slipper. If you feel desperate, like you're pushing or scared to hear no….you won't attract much.

Law of Attraction brings people into your sales funnel. When you are super excited about your offerings, you feel good talking about them, dig your pricing, and only focus on working with your ideal peeps.

Jeanna Gabellini is a Master Business Coach who assists high-achieving entrepreneurs, corporate leaders & their teams to leverage fun, systems and intentionality for high-octane results. She co-authored *Life Lessons for Mastering the Law of Attraction* with Jack Canfield, Mark Victor Hansen and Eva Gregory. Get your complimentary Audio CD "Transforming from Chaotic Entrepreneur to Conscious Leader"

at http://www.MasterPeaceCoaching.com/freecd.

* * *

In order to do the tough marketing tasks, uncover your inspiration. Find the source of your energy.

Where Do You Get Your Inspiration?

Until now, I have never written about this personal detail in any book.

Do I have your attention?

My close friends have seen that I have a couple of items that have the "S" shield of Superman. No, I don't wear tshirts with a comic book character on them. It is the "S" shield that inspires me. To me it means: hope, compassion, nurturing, strength—oh—and flying.

Your marketing needs to inspire you! When you hand out your business card, there must be no hesitation. We need you to make your marketing materials into things that fill you with good energy.

For example, more than ten years ago, I wrote a book and a dear friend suggested I call it *Communicate to Win.* I felt okay about the title (as I mentioned earlier).

Later, I renamed the book *Be Heard and Be Trusted* (now in its third edition). Now that inspires me! I help people be heard. And I support people expressing how positive and trustworthy they are. (You can see the helping and nurturing aspect as mentioned with the "S" shield above.)

So ... Where do you get your inspiration?

* * *

Inspiration can be a first step. Then you need to take action.

A Celebration of Your Life Transformed—Really?

Have you done some of the Action Steps in this book? Okay. Take a deep breath. Some readers will just read a book like this. Instead, I invite you to do something.

Take just 20 seconds and write something down in response to a question. You have just tripled the value of this book to your life. How do you enjoy a life transformed? You take one step forward at a time.

Recently, I was offered a new class to teach at the university where I currently teach eight classes. How did that happen? Some months earlier, I heard that a new department was forming. I went directly to the leader of that new department and expressed my experience and qualifications for the job. That is marketing. She can trust that I will do an excellent job of teaching the students skills that they'll use for a life-long career.

So now, your chance to transform your life begins with one step forward:

What do you want?

What do you want to feel?

What will your new life look like [after you effectively market your product or service]? How will your new life feel?

What will make all of your marketing efforts feel worth it?

That's it—answer the questions. Your transformation beings now.

* * *

When you focus on transformation, pain becomes less of an issue. Your good feelings overpower potential pain.

Points to Remember:

*** Secret #7: People procrastinate because they anticipate pain.**

*** Your Countermeasure:**

Use a multi-faceted approach to overcome procrastination due to anticipating pain:

- Uncover your inspiration.
- Find ways to feel good about both selling and marketing.
- Set inspiring goals.
- Transform "work hard" to "work joy."

* * * * * *

Secret #8: People procrastinate because they lack clarity.

What is clarity? *The American Heritage Dictionary of the English Language* defines *clarity* as "1. Clearness of appearance: *the clarity of the mountain air.* and 2. Clearness of thought or style; lucidity: *writes with clarity and perception.*"

People who lack clarity are tentative. Recall any great leader. Did that leader wave in some general direction and say, "Okay, we're going to go somewhere that-a-way. I'm not really sure"?

Instead, we need you to be clear in your purpose and direction like a ship captain who knows exactly what latitude and longitude he or she is navigating to.

You, as a strong marketer, need clarity that can arise from knowing answers to these questions:

1) Who is your target market?
2) Where are they hurting?
3) What do they desperately want?
4) How is your competition failing them?
5) What would surpass their expectations?
6) What would surprise and delight them?
7) What is the essence of your product/service?
8) How does your product/service provide a transformation for your client?*

* Elsewhere in this book, I talk about how a transformation is what the client really wants. For example, a book or workshop can guide a person to experience new confidence. Becoming a confident person is the transformation.

9-Minute Method (#8): Build Your High Value Description

Why You Need to Do This:

Focus on something that customers have said when they were pleased with your product or service. From this foundation, we will build your High Value Description (HVD), which is your answer when people ask you, "So what exactly do you do?"

Here are examples:

- "My clients say that I really help them be calm and loose so that they perform at their best when it counts." (sports psychologist)
- "My clients say that I provide attention-getting logos and packaging that get customers energized to buy their products." (graphic artist)

You notice that the above statements clearly express the *high value benefits* that the sports psychologist and graphic artist provide.

When you boil down what you do into exactly what your clients most value, you're ready to form your marketing campaign around that focal point.

The Exercise:

In the next nine minutes, we're going to use a device that will likely warm up your memories. Write down *what you would want clients to say*. You are starting with your imagination. You do *not* have to wrack your brain to remember something from the past.

Once your brain starts looking at ideas of what you would want to hear, often your brain also serves up positive memories.

Take those positive memories of delighted customer comments and use them as a foundation of your High Value

Description. Write down three quick versions of your High Value Description.

Now, you can build your marketing campaign on the benefits that clients have experienced.

* * *

To be a strong marketer, you often need to lead contractors. Learn how to be effective and decisive through Mark Sanborn's following insights.

The Decisive Leader

by Mark Sanborn

The problem most leaders face isn't being more decisive–it is being informed enough to make a decision. They waffle because they don't understand the problem or situation, haven't framed it well or haven't thoroughly considered the options for addressing it.

Here's what to do when facing a problem or decision:

First, define it.

Unclear problems cause unclear solutions (the same is true for opportunities). Make sure you can answer: what is the real problem or opportunity here?

To answer that question, follow the resources: how is this situation costing us money or time (in terms of direct or opportunity cost)? Know the difference between an inconvenience (not particularly costly) and a true problem (expensive enough to solve).

Second, look for the any opportunity the problem might represent.

Here's an example:

As YouTube became really successful, they realized they had a copyright problem. Much of the material on their site was protected and they were obligated (because of lawsuits) to take it down. But the copyrighted stuff drove much of the traffic on the site. The solution: they developed a program that notified copyright holders as soon as their protected material was posted and offered to remove it. The opportunity: they also offered the holders half the revenue from any ads alongside the protected video AND the opportunity to use the video for promotional purposes. Now that program accounts for a third of YouTube's revenue.

Third, ask who, what and how?

WHO is most informed about the problem or apprised of the situation? Identify them as such. Ask WHAT they perceive the problem to be and HOW they suggest solving it. Having several good conversations will go a long way towards getting the information you need.

Now, generate options. The quicker you come up with a solution, the less likely it is the best solution. Look a second or third time at what you could do.

Finally, pick the solution that offers the best long-term fix.

Any problem that doesn't stay solved wasn't solved correctly to begin with. And no opportunity can be maximized without a great plan.

* * * * * *

12 Productivity Tips

1. Carry a notebook everywhere because you need to capture important ideas. Fight boredom with creative writing, vision casting and planning.

2. Get clear on the results you want to create before you think about strategies and tactics.

3. Know what you do best and what only you can do. Those are the things that should get first priority on your schedule.

4. Be willing to do what is necessary but don't do what you're not best at unless it is absolutely necessary. Delegate what you can.

5. Don't try to outsource your creativity. Ask for input and ideas, but take responsibility for your own creative output.

6. Think again. And again. Spending money without forethought is expensive.

7. Know yourself. Schedule according to your style and preferences.

8. Don't do what is easy, do what is important.

9. Have a few priorities but a long to do list.

10. Write it down as soon as you think it.

11. Don't do things out of obligation. If it doesn't represent an opportunity, why are you doing it?

12. Question for the beginning of the day: what are the most important things I want to accomplish today? Question for the end of the day: what did I accomplish today?

Mark Sanborn is the president of Sanborn & Associates, Inc., an idea lab for leadership development. Leadershipgurus.net lists him as one of the top 30 leadership experts in the world. Mark has authored 9 books and more than two dozen videos and audio training programs. He has presented over 2200 speeches and seminars in every state and 12 foreign countries. His book, *The Fred Factor: How Passion in Your Work and Life Can Turn the Ordinary into the Extraordinary* has sold over 1.1 million copies. His latest books are *Up, Down or Sideways: How to Succeed When Times Are Good, Bad, or In Between; You Don't Need a Title to be a Leader: How Anyone, Anywhere Can Make a Positive Difference* and *The Encore Effect: How to Achieve Remarkable Performance in Anything You Do*. Mark is a past president of the National Speakers Association and winner of The Cavett. In 2007 Mark was awarded The Ambassador of Free Enterprise Award by Sales & Marketing

Executives International. MarkSanborn.com

* * *

This chapter is about gaining clarity. When it comes to writing blog articles and other forms of marketing, it helps to have a system for writing. Paul Gillin now shares his insights.

Five Tips to Make Your Writing Sparkle
by Paul Gillin

Now that we're all publishers, writing has become a core skill for marketers. I love good writing, and whenever I get the chance to teach it, I share these five tricks I've learned to make anyone's writing better.

1. Write in Pictures. Former *Wall Street Journal* page one feature writer Bill Blundell used that phrase in a seminar some 15 years ago, and I've never forgotten it. It's the single best piece of writing advice I've ever had.

Human beings think visually. The words we read continually conjure up images in our mind. So why settle for ordinary words when vivid images are available?

Consider this passage from a *Journal* story from two years ago about the declining popularity of Grape Nuts cereal. Describing the factory in which the century-old breakfast staple is made, reporter Barry Newman writes (emphasis added):

"All day every day, objects with the proportions of **hewn firewood** and the heft of **cinder blocks hurtle** along a conveyor, **dive** into a steel chute, **disappear** down a black hole — and emit what sounds like a **startled scream**."

Each of the bolded terms creates a mental association that

makes the scene come to life. Words like "hurtle" and "dive" are so much more descriptive than "travel" and "fall." These are words everyone knows; we just don't think to use them.

2. Tell stories. In writing *The Joy of Geocaching* with Dana two years ago, I had the chance to use one of the best opening sentences I've ever written: "In early 2003 Ed Manley decided to kill himself."

The following paragraphs went on to tell about an injured and embittered veteran who discovered a game that gave his life new purpose. It was a powerful story that encapsulated the curious appeal of geocaching in a way that no statistics could have matched.

Storytelling is the oldest form of human communication and the most instinctively effective. They hit us in our gut. They are one of the most effective tools we have to grab a reader's attention. Tell them whenever possible.

3. Get angry. Newspaper columnists use this trick all the time. We write best about topics that stir our passion. You may think your situation doesn't lend itself to such emotion, but with a little imagination, you can get angry about even seemingly mundane things: the way people behave in meetings, the antics of an industry standards group or the way a company treats its customers.

Getting angry doesn't mean going on a tirade or hurling insults. That's embarrassing. Anger is better expressed with irony, sarcasm, counterpoint or wry condescension. The more eloquent your words, the more appealing your message. If you make people laugh, all the better.

One of my favorite angry writers is the *Baltimore Sun's* John McIntyre, whose You Don't Say blog should be in every writer's RSS feed. In a recent entry condemning restroom devices that periodically emit a spritz of perfume, he wrote,

"It does nothing to cancel out the underlying smell of the premises, merely adding one offensive aroma atop another. It's rather as if someone went to the zoo and spritzed the bonobos with Dollar Store perfume."

If you can send your readers scurrying to Google to look up "bonobo," you've won.

4. Remove Unnecessary Words. Do you ever get memos about how someone "facilitated the process" instead of just "did?" Is there ever any reason to use the phrase, "We all know that…?" Have you received an e-mail stating that "Greater emphasis and guidance was placed on ensuring…" when it could have said, "We stressed…?"

Verbose writing and passive voice are drilled into us beginning in junior high school, and we suffer the consequences of this injustice every day. We don't always have the time to tighten our messages, but it's a service to readers when we do.

Try this with your next essay or staff memo: Re-read what you've written and remove every unnecessary term. Change passive voice to active: Instead of "succeeded in accomplishing," try "did." Substitute short words for long ones. See how many words you can remove without diluting the meaning. You'll be surprised.

5. Surprise Your Reader. Writing coach Don Fry calls these "gold coins." They're the little nuggets of information that delight and reward readers for staying with us. Or they may just make us laugh.

Consider this passage from *The Rubber Room,* a withering assault on the way the United Federation of Teachers protects some of New York City's worst educators. Describing a competency hearing for fifth-grade teacher Lucienne Mohammed, Steven Brill writes that her case "is likely to take between forty and forty-five hearing days—

eight times as long as the average criminal trial in the United States." That little nugget of comparative data validates the point of the story more effectively than any quote from a frustrated administrator ever could. Brill did a little extra work to make his point a lot more powerful.

Or how about this gem from *Why Craigslist Is Such a Mess,* Gary Wolf's wonderful exploration of the enigmatic classified ad site in the August 2009 *Wired:*

"Jim Buckmaster is tall and thin, [Craig] Newmark is short and round, and when they stand together they look like a binary number."

I laughed out loud at that. It was a reward for reading the 3,000 words that came before it (which were also very good).

The three feature articles I've cited above are fantastic examples of great writing. Here are a couple of others that I've used in recent classes:

Fatal Distraction: Forgetting a Child in the Backseat of a Car Is a Horrifying Mistake. Is It a Crime? This gut-wrenching 8,700-word feature story in the *Washington Post* won the Pulitzer Prize in 2009. Read it and you'll see why. It will touch your soul.

The No-Stats All-Star – Michael Lewis' profile of Shane Battier, a seemingly unremarkable NBA forward who raises every team he plays for to a higher level continually delights us with gold coins and features one of the best conclusions I've ever read.

Paul Gillin is the author of *Social Marketing to the Business Customer* and *The New Influencers and Secrets of Social Media Marketing.*

Paul Gillin Communications

Content Strategies for Social Media

4 Thurber St., Framingham, MA 01702

508-202-9807 office, 781-929-6754 mobile
email: paul@gillin.com web: gillin.com
Twitter: pgillin, LinkedIn: paulgillin

* * *

Now we move from writing skills to another element of marketing: *identify your competition*—their strengths and weaknesses. And identify how you can make a unique platform and serve your customers.

Let's begin with a quote:

"I have been up against tough competition all my life. I wouldn't know how to get along without it."—Walt Disney

What possible good could Walt Disney be hinting at? His comment implies that competition, for a number of entrepreneurs, spurs them to greater quality and better accomplishments.

Research Your Competition

Some people say, "I'm not competitive." That may be true. But denying your competition's presence is similar to denying that the sun exists because clouds obscure your vision on an overcast day.

Competition has an undeniable presence and impact on your marketing. We'll focus on three areas so that you can prepare your marketing campaign to deal with competition.

1. Play the Role of Your Customer Doing a Search
2. View Competition Like an Olympic Athlete
3. Take the "Grow Rich in a Niche" Approach

1. Play the Role of Your Customer Doing a Search

A number of people say, "I do not know how to conduct formal research of the competition." If that's holding you back, consider starting in a simple manner. Just pretend to be a potential customer and imagine how you would find a vendor like you. What would they do? They'd ask friends, or most likely, they'd type into Google Search a few keywords. For example, Sheree wanted a personal coach. So she typed in Google search "personal coach San Francisco."

There are thousands of personal coaches and, in a sense, they're all in competition for the same client pool. In particular, many personal coaches use the telephone for client sessions. So your coach could be anywhere in the world. However, each personal coach is an individual, and they have certain focus areas. Not all of them have attended the same certification courses. Some specialize in executive training while others have a focus on rising women executives. The question of marketing is to stand out of a big crowd of competitors. I like to say to my clients who are striving for success: *"To stand out, find out what you stand for."* What does that mean? It means that when you find out what means so much to you, you start to express something unique. When you do something unique, your competition fades away because no one will be doing what you do exactly the way that you do it. If someone tries to compare music by the Beatles with that by Whitney Houston, it's not really about competition. It's about the listeners' preference.

Find your personal gift and unique contribution. For example, Maria wants to be known as the preeminent coach to women executives. It would do her a lot of good to have a website focused on "coaching for executive women." Perhaps, she might choose a URL like "CoachforExecutiveWomen.com" or something in that vein. Why? Such a specific URL could help her get more web visitors as search engines find her website.

2. View Competition Like an Olympic Athlete

Olympic athletes frequently develop friendships with their competitors. Why? Numerous athletes say something like: "I ran my best race against George." Competition raises the game of all of the competitors. My point is that it is empowering to look on the whole process of competition as something to improve everyone's performance. On the other hand, it can be disempowering to look upon competition as "a war." Why? Because battle causes fatigue. But incentive to do better can actually be a source of personal energy.

So don't let fear about competition stop you or paralyze you. Use competition as a springboard to your preparation. How? When you look around and see other companies that are accomplishing good work, let that be a form of inspiration. Ask yourself, "How can I do excellent work, too? How can I do something different that helps me stand out?"

And the good news is that business does not require the exclusive reward that an Olympian seeks: one Gold Medal. The truth is you are in your own unique, personal race. No one else can be you.

Here's another fact about marketing. As you go along, the marketplace starts to tell you what people want from you. For example, I had written four books that were made available on Amazon.com before I released *Darkest Secrets of Persuasion and Seduction Masters: How to Protect Yourself and Turn the Power to Good*. This book sold so well that I was inspired to write other books in the *Darkest Secrets . . . How to Protect Yourself* series on negotiation, spiritual seduction, acting, film direction, and business communication. The marketplace had spoken. I was in a "new race"—one that I had created with the first "Darkest Secrets" book.

Find your unique "foot race."

3. Take the "Grow Rich in a Niche" Approach

Novice marketers have a typical answer to the question: "Who is this product for?" "Everybody!" the novice says.

That approach is not helpful. Why? By trying to serve everyone, you often water down a product so much that you're not saying or doing anything with real impact. Here's an example. Let's say someone wanted to devise a superhero that would debut in a graphic novel, then would work its way to a franchise of feature films. If the creator of said superhero tried to pile together the characteristics of Batman and Superman, it's likely that such a mashed-together character would appeal to no one!

Batman has fans who relate to his tragic past and his determined vigilantism. Fans of Superman have traditionally appreciated the uplifting and positive nature of this hero. A number of individuals have said that Superman is the "blue boy scout" representing hope. The lesson we get from this example is: Pick something specific. If you want to create a dark character, go ahead. If you want something lighter, like the refreshing film *Marvel's The Avengers,* go in that direction. That's the point: pick a specific direction. We can see this in the creation of female characters, too. A rebellious Catwoman and a righteous Wonder Woman. This is on my mind because I've written three female leading characters for my graphic novel *TimePulse.*

To "Grow Rich in a Niche," focus on defining a small group that you can truly serve. If you try to serve too wide a group, you'll fail them. Why? Your material will be too general. For example, near the beginning of his speaking career, Mark Victor Hansen focused on speaking to chiropractors. To do a great speech, he needed to customize his talk to his particular audience. Providing one "generic talk" would not do.

If you try to avoid offending anyone, you will not be saying anything (as I mentioned earlier) that has high impact and big value. So be bold and narrowly define your target market. Why is that "bold"? Because many novice entrepreneurs attempt to have a "big net" to catch "many types of people." They think they'll be "safer" that way. Instead, the "Grow Rich in a Niche" approach is about focusing your attention on a small group and so thoroughly helping them, that you become the preeminent choice of vendor for them.

Answer these questions for yourself to focus and refine your marketing message:

a) What is different about my product from that of my competitors?

b) How do I fulfill an unserved need?

c) What makes me both unique and unusually trustworthy to my customers?

d) Where are my competitors strong and I am weak?

e) Where are my competitors weak and I am strong? Can I get stronger in this area?

For example, there are hundreds of books on marketing. How could I stand out from the competition? How could I focus on a niche-element? For this book, I wanted to focus on some aspect of marketing that had been ignored—procrastination. Other books merely list marketing methods, but such lists do not guide the person to push past internal blocks and procrastination. On the other hand, this book takes procrastination head-on.

In summary, we've discussed three areas related to competition:

1. Play the Role of Your Customer Doing a Search
2. View Competition Like an Olympic Athlete

3. Take the "Grow Rich in a Niche" Approach

Become skilled in identifying your competitors. Assess their strengths and weaknesses. Then find a gap in what they're doing. Do they fail their customers in some way? That is the gap you're looking for. And, in essence, grow rich in a niche.

Points to Remember:

*** Secret #8: People procrastinate because they lack clarity.**

*** Your Countermeasure:**

Begin to gain clarity about your marketing campaign by answering these questions:

1) Who is your target market?
2) Where are they hurting?
3) What do they desperately want?
4) How is your competition failing them?
5) What would surpass their expectations?
6) What would surprise and delight them?
7) What is the essence of your product/service?
8) How does your product/service provide a transformation for your client?*

* About transformation: Does the person become confident? Does she now have the skills to take her business to a higher level? Does he feel energized to take action?

* * * * * *

Secret #9: People procrastinate because they think they're going to fail.

Imagine this. You can set things up in which you do not fail, that is you gain some headway—no matter how the marketing campaign turns out. How? You make sure your message reflects the positive value of what you're marketing. You create your positive brand.

This principle even relates to ethics in advertising. Why? When you do marketing and advertising, make sure that you avoid doing anything that tarnishes your reputation (that would be real failure).

Being Good Means "Good for Your Business"

Have you heard about the topic "ethics in advertising"? Long-lasting companies build their business on long-term relationships with customers. Ethical advertising opens the door maintaining the relationships throughout the years.

"Genuine gifts, given with the right intent and a respectful posture meet our sniff test," wrote Seth Godin, known as the most influential business blogger in the world. Seth consistently holds the place as one of the twenty-five most widely read bloggers in the English language. About gifts, Seth also wrote: "If I create an idea, the Internet makes it possible for that gift to spread everywhere, quite quickly, at no cost to me. Digital gifts, ideas that spread—these allow the artist to be far more generous than he could ever be in an analog world."

What kind of gifts? A song, an e-book, a recording of a speech, a photo, a poem, a free chapter—it's up to you. YouTube.com is a compelling and influential outlet that allows people to post their song, video or recording of a speech. A number of people surf YouTube. com and discover new offerings everyday, and YouTube.com has reportedly over one billion views per day.

Here's an example of how an offering on YouTube.com took off. First, the song may have been a clever way to complain. But the humor and musicality of the work became a form of gift. A singer/songwriter Dave Carroll posted a song "United Breaks Guitars" detailing how his Taylor guitar was broken by United Airlines personnel and no one stepped forward to help the situation. As I write these words, the song/video has been viewed 14.4 million times. My colleagues have said, "That song and video placed Dave Carroll on the map. I bet it helped his career."

Let's continue this conversation along the lines of advertising. How do we express good ethical behavior in advertising?

First, realize every consumer uses the "sniff test" on every bit of advertising. It's a self-defense reflex. Consumers seek to protect themselves from poor products that waste their money.

Second, begin your process with the right intent with your advertising: Sell something that will help the buyer!

Third, have your advertising include a respectful posture. How? Don't lie, exaggerate, or "bait and switch." Consumers hate being promised one product (the bait) and being told that another product (the switch) will suit them just as well—since the "bait-product" is somehow no longer available.

Do tell the truth. Substantiate your claims with proof. Disclose your guarantee or warranty. Have real people give true testimonials.

Use that respectful posture in advertising and you can begin long-term relationships with customers.

Another way to do good with advertising and public relations efforts is to connect your product with doing something benevolent. For example, authors Jay Conrad Levinson and Shel Horowitz announced "a portion of the authors' net profits from the book *Guerrilla Marketing Goes Green* launch will be donated to Green America (greenamericatoday.org), a not-for-profit organization founded in 1982 (as Co-op America) with a mission to harness economic power—the strength of consumers, investors, businesses, and the marketplace—to create a socially just and environmentally sustainable society."

A personal example: My family counts on Walt Disney Resorts to provide top notch service and friendly, courteous interactions. My sweetheart said, "Let's go to Alaska." I replied, "Okay. Let's take the Disney Cruise."

Customers appreciate businesses who are ethical in advertising and customer service. My vacation example shows how consumers will buy again and again from businesses who are trustworthy. Be reliable. Be consistent. It is simply good business.

* * *

Be sure to guard your reputation. Then, to keep up your own morale, become proactive in redefining what "failure" means to you personally.

9-Minute Method (#9): Redefine "Failure"

Why You Need to Do This:

Years ago, I had two marketing campaigns that yielded just a couple of sales. Were they failures? Not if I learned something. You can bet that I paid close attention and modified my approach the next time.

We'll focus on three areas for redefining failure. Why is this useful? If you know that you'll find a way to win, to get better each time you do a marketing campaign, then you can quiet down the fear of failure. And you'll avoid letting such fear paralyze you and prevent you from taking positive action.

Here are the three areas for redefining failure:

1) Identify how you "took ground."

2) Celebrate How You "Sharpened the Saw" (Refined Your Marketing Message).

3) Focus on "You always win when you learn something."

1) Identify how you "took ground."

In a battle, sometimes an army tries to take ground, that is, to gain control of some territory. Every time you go into the marketplace, you can take some ground. How? Reach out to your target market. Researchers demonstrate that it often takes five connections with a potential customer before she says, "Yes. I'll buy that." So if you send out an enewsletter with a coupon, you have accomplished one of the five connections. To do better, see if you can design your marketing campaign to have multiple connections. You can send an enewsletter with a coupon, you can email a brief reminder with a link to your webpage with the coupon and an additional special benefit (perhaps, a free report), and you can call the person on the phone. That campaign has three connections to the potential buyer. Good plan!

So when you say that you "took ground" or "made one of the connections to the buyer"— you have NOT failed. You have made a step forward.

2) Celebrate How You "Sharpened the Saw" (Refined Your Marketing Message).

Author Stephen R. Covey referred to "sharpen the saw."

He repeated Abraham Lincoln's comment: "If I had eight hours to chop down a tree, I'd spend six hours sharpening my ax." How does this apply to marketing? Your marketing message is your ax. Each time you enter the marketplace, you naturally refine your marketing message just to get your message out through whatever media you use (social media, direct mail, enewsletters, and more).

So you do not fail because with each marketing campaign you hone and sculpt your marketing message. And you sharpen your skills at deploying that message. The more you make those calls or write those enewsletters, the better you get at them. That's progress. That's a win! (And that's redefining failure.)

Here's an example of sharpening your saw (your message). Bestselling author John Gray started giving presentations on the differences between men and women. He kept refining his message until eight years later he launched a book with the title *Men Are From Mars, Women are From Venus.* Finally, he had a title that encapsulated his concepts and that captured the imagination of millions of readers—at least 7 million readers! This was the launching pad for several bestselling books, certification courses for coaches using his methodology, and the rest of his Mars/Venus empire.

3) Focus on "You always win when you learn something."

One of my clients only gained a couple of sales when she launched her book as a paperback. She asked, "Should I try this book as an ebook?"

As we went through her results, some concerns about the title came up. I suggested, "How about coming up with a new title and then seeing if the ebook sells well under that new title?"

Did my client "fail" by launching her paperback book under a faulty title? Not really. When she takes a strategic long view of her career, she understands how this product, title, and marketing campaign have enriched her knowledge and wisdom to become a strong marketer. Instead of failing, she "won" by honing her message as she refined the description of her material on the back cover of her book.

She also won by writing the book in the first place. One of the best ways to truly learn material is to prepare to teach someone else. My client now *knows* her message, and she can repurpose her text as an ebook under the new title.

The Exercise:

Grab a sheet of paper and write down the following three topic areas—and leave space below each heading so that you can write your answer immediately below:

1) Identify how you "took ground."

2) Celebrate How You "Sharpened the Saw" (Refined Your Marketing Message).

3) Focus on "You always win when you learn something."

In the next nine minutes, brainstorm and write your ideas that are appropriate below each topic area.

Once you have completed this exercise, you have a new perspective on your product and the marketing campaign. You get a new viewpoint, one of long-term career strategies. In this manner, you become a strong marketer.

* * *

Some people are so afraid of failure that they have trouble sleeping.

How You Can Be a Marketer Who Goes to Sleep Happy

Ever have too many thoughts racing around in your head? Have difficulty falling to sleep? How I could have used this next method when I was in college!

While in college, I would go to sleep disappointed. It seemed like my to-do list was never getting smaller. I felt on some level like a failure every night just before my head hit the pillow. And I wrote some of the most downhearted letters to my then-girlfriend. (Note to self: do not write an email or letter when feeling down. Second note to self: write the email in MS Word so I do not accidentally send an inappropriate email message.)

Here's the solution I have found:

Write for 2 minutes in a personal Daily Journal of Blessings and Victories. A blessing is something good that appears, like a friend calls up out of the blue. A victory is something that you have accomplished like: "Came up with 3 possible designs for the logo."

So, as an effective marketer, be sure to write down your incremental accomplishments before you go to sleep. You can see and feel that you're making progress.

After my two-minute writing session in my Daily Journal, I grab a 3x5 card. For one minute, I write my next day's Top-Six-Targets. These are my most important tasks for the next day; and this plan serves as my "marching orders" for the next day.

Ahhhhh! Now I can go to sleep happy with my blessings and accomplishments. And my mind is cleared of worry about what I need to do the next day. This process protects my energy. Try this process, and you'll thank me.

* * *

You need sleep so that your brain functions well.

Researchers note that higher brain functions suffer when one misses too much sleep. Now, we'll explore Noah St. John's system for writing better content. By applying his methods, many of us will start to relax about the necessary element of marketing: good writing.

3 Simple Rules to Create Content Better, Faster, Easier
by Noah St. John

Have you ever felt "stuck" when trying to come up with articles, videos, blog posts, or social media content? If you said "no", you're either Stephen King or a big ol' liar. The truth is, most of us know all too well the feeling of "staring at a computer screen and mind freezing." Here are three simple rules to increase your "likes and shares" for your articles, videos, blog posts, and social media content:

Rule #1. The Audience Is Listening—To Themselves.

Who would you rather go to dinner with: someone who talks incessantly about themselves, or someone who's genuinely interested in YOU?

One of the reasons we get "stuck" is because we are literally stuck on ourselves. Next time you sit down to create an article, video, blog post, or social media content, think about the people you want to impact.

More specifically, picture a SPECIFIC PERSON in your mind; for example, one of your Core Customers, clients or prospects who you have actually communicated with recently. If that person had hired you to give them advice, what would you say to them?

Then:

1. Write a brief, concise, informative message.
2. Use clear language that gets your point across

quickly—don't obfuscate, equivocate, or use words like "obfuscate" or "equivocate."

3. Don't always talk about how great your product or service is. Of course, there are times you DO need to talk about how great your product or service is. Just not every time.

Remember, people will like you more when you demonstrate that you're just as concerned about THEIR problems as you are about your own. And people do business with people they like.

Rule #2. Address Your Core Customer's Pain AND Ambition.

Question: What's the greatest motivator in the world? Answer: Pain.

Why? Biologically speaking, any organism must avoid pain in order to not die. That's why most marketers focus the majority of their messages on their prospects' PAIN.

However, when ALL you talk about is pain, your messages become like Johnny One-Note:

"Aaaaaaaaaaaaaaaaaaaaaaaaaaaaaahhhhhhhhhhhh!"

It gets a little boring.

So, when creating any online content, also address your Core Customer's AMBITION—their dreams, hopes and desires.

For example: When you follow Rule #1 and really put yourself in your Core Customer's shoes, imagine what their day is like. (You may not have to imagine much, because odds are you're a lot like them.)

To address pain, ask questions like: "What am I afraid of? What is hurting me or scaring me right now? What's my biggest frustration?"

But then, also ask questions to elicit your Core Customer's

AMBITION: "What do I really, really WANT? What's my dream or big goal? What do I think is JUST out of reach that I would really like to have?"

Address your Core Customer's pain AND their ambition, and people will be more likely to respond positively to your messages.

Rule #3: Leave 'Em Wanting More.

A man was leaving an auditorium in the middle of a speaker's oration. A woman who was just coming in asked him: "Oh, is the speaker finished?" He replied, "The speaker was finished a half hour ago. He just hasn't stopped talking."

A good rule of thumb is to keep your online content between 500-1,200 words. In the immortal words of Paul Hogan: "When you're onstage, remember the three G's: Be gracious. Be grateful. Get off."

Whenever you post online content—including articles, videos, blog posts, and social media content—never forget that you are "onstage." The more gracious and grateful you are—and the quicker you get off, after having made your point—the more likely people will be to respond to your messages.

The best speakers, writers, communicators and content creators always leave something to their audience's imagination.

Noah's Note: People do business with people they like. Use these 3 simple rules to increase your "Likeability" as well as your bank account.

Noah St. John is the inventor of Afformations (r) and bestselling author of *Permission to Succeed* (r) and *The Secret Code of Success: 7 Hidden Steps to More Wealth and Happiness*

(HarperCollins). He's the world's most-quoted expert on how to dump your head trash. Noah has been featured in over 2,000 media outlets including CNN, ABC, NBC, CBS, Fox, National Public Radio, *PARADE, Woman's Day, Los Angeles Business Journal, Washington Post, Chicago Sun-Times, Selling Power, Southwest Spirit, Bottom Line/Personal,* and *The Huffington Post.*

With no formal education in business and a vision to empower millions of people worldwide, he launched SuccessClinic.com in 1997 with a mission to teach entrepreneurs around the world how to get unstuck. Noah's books have been translated into twelve languages, including Japanese, French, German, Russian, Arabic, and Mandarin Chinese.

Fun fact: Noah once won an all-expenses-paid trip to Hawaii on the game show Concentration hosted by Alex Trebek, where he missed winning a new car by three seconds. (Note: He had not yet discovered *The Secret Code of Success.*)

Visit www.NoahStJohn.com for FREE video training on how to have more abundance and well-being in just 5 minutes a day.

* * *

In the book I co-authored, *Full Strength Marketing,* I expanded on two types of schedules. You'll need such schedules for preparing your marketing materials.

Schedule Version #1: The week-by-week schedule

The week-by-week schedule begins with the date you generate ideas or hire a designer, and continues until your pieces are in the customer's hands.

The sample week-by-week schedule flows as follows:

Example Schedule

Objective:

Target dates

Generate ideas or hire designer	June 1
Talk over concepts, costs and schedule	June 10
Talk to copywriter & get costs & schedule	June 15
Choose photography and illustrations	June 20
Deliver writing to designer	June 30
Review printed pieces	July 6
Final edit and copy approval	July 12
Printer	July 15
Delivery	July 18
Have in customers' hands	July 21

Schedule Version #2: The Backward Schedule

The backward schedule will begin with the date that you want your printed pieces to be in the customers' hands, and you work backward from that date.

Example Backward Schedule

Objective:

Time required, target dates

Have in customers' hands	July 21
Delivery	3 days, July 18
Printer	3 days, July 15
Final edit and copy approval	3 days, July 12
Review printed pieces	6 days, July 6
Deliver writing to designer	one wk, June 30
Choose photography and illustrations	10 days, June 20
Talk to copywriter and get costs & schedule	5 days, June 15
Talk over concepts, costs and schedule	5 days, June 10
Generate ideas or hire designer	10 days, June 1

How to Choose the Schedule to Use

My team uses both schedules. We begin with the week-by-week schedule because it's intuitive: We all picture the future as ahead of us. Then we refine our scheduling by drafting a backwards schedule. In using both versions of schedules, we uncover hidden details.

* * *

Before we leave this chapter about fearing failure, I want to give you an insight that has saved me thousands of dollars.

Early in my business ownership career, I hired a contractor to write some marketing material. She was paid by the hour. After a week or two, she presented me with a large bill. She had honestly worked a lot of hours, and I paid her for them.

But I learned an important lesson: Put a cap (or limit) on expenses. If you do not have a cap on the project budget, you might get a bad surprise in that the professional has devoted too much time and incurred costs that are too high. Protect yourself. You can say something like: "This project cannot exceed $1500. So keep me posted. If this project seems to start to go over budget, I require that you and I talk about this. I may need to cut something out."

Fear of failure paralyzes some people, but not you. In this chapter I have shared methods so that you can improve your perspective. Remember it's not a failure when you learn something and then change your behavior for the next marketing campaign.

Points to Remember:

*** Secret #9: People procrastinate because they think**

they're going to fail.

*** Your Countermeasure:**

Be proactive. Do *not* accept your own first thoughts and feelings about what might be a failure. Instead, look deeper. Redefine failure by using these methods:

1) Identify how you "took ground."
2) Celebrate How You "Sharpened the Saw" (Refined Your Marketing Message).
3) Focus on "You always win when you learn something."

* * * * * *

Secret #10: Many people fail to evaluate the results of a marketing campaign.

Why do people often fail to evaluate the results of a marketing campaign? Simple: They want to avoid more pain. More pain? Yes, they're already feeling vague pain because they probably took a first glance and felt uncomfortable with the results they received.

Earlier in this book, we talked about procrastination that arises in an effort to avoid pain. That was about not even getting started. Now, this following section is different because we're at the other end of a marketing campaign, the closing.

9-Minute Method (#10): Triple Positive Evaluation

Why You Need to Do This:

Here's how you can plan your evaluation of a marketing campaign AND keep up your morale. The reason for the Triple Positive Evaluation is that many of us normally gravitate to the "bad news." Often, we had high expectations for many sales, and reality came in at a lower number of sales.

It truly helps to use the following three-step process to face the truth and take care of yourself simultaneously.

Step One (Positive Evaluation #1): Identify your goals on three levels

Many marketers only measure their effectiveness based on a dollar amount. That's too limiting. You can include these levels: a) dollar amount we earned, b) how we served people, c) how we positioned ourselves for more and better results. Earlier in this book, we discussed positioning, that is, creating an image in the minds of your target market. If you effectively accomplish positioning, you are likely priming your target market to buy in the future.

Step Two (Positive Evaluation #2): Find some way to praise yourself

What did you do right? What worked? What did you learn? Remember, you acted with courage. You did something. I call that "better than zero." An old phrase holds: "Success goes to the activist." Praise yourself for being active. Praise yourself for trying something, learning, and positioning yourself to do better next time. Take this further: *Write down* all of your praise on a sheet of paper as part of "Positive Evaluation #2."

Step Three (Positive Evaluation #3): Find the Lesson and Place It into Your "Next Time Plan"

Every marketing campaign yields lessons. Find them. Write them down. Place them into your plan for next time. I remember a powerful comment bestselling author Marianne

Williamson's father said. Marianne spent $10,000 on a particular event that turned out in a disappointing fashion. Did her father say "Oh no, what a mess you made"? No! Instead, her father put his arm around her shoulders and said, "You can absorb this." In essence, he expressed his faith that Marianne was more than this temporary setback.

My mentor, Dottie Walters, speaker and author, once told me: "Failure? I never encountered it. All I ever met were temporary setbacks."

As an entrepreneur, I have produced many products and marketing campaigns. And I've learned from each one!

As I wrote in my book *Be Heard and Be Trusted, 3rd Edition: Harvest the wisdom from an error and you are twice blessed: you won't repeat the error and you know what to compensate for.*

The Exercise:

Now, it's your turn. Grab three sheets of paper and label them with the following Three Steps. Leave space so you can write below each heading.

Step One (Positive Evaluation #1): Identify your goals on three levels

- Level A: Dollar amount we earned.
- Level B: How we served people.
- Level C: How we positioned ourselves for more and better results.

Step Two (Positive Evaluation #2): Find some way to praise yourself

Write your answers to these questions: What did you do right? What worked?

Step Three (Positive Evaluation #3): Find the Lesson and Place It into Your "Next Time Plan"

Take notes about what you learned and what you intend

to repeat or do differently for your next marketing campaign. Prepare a file folder on your computer or in a binder to store your notes about what you learned.

Now, in the next nine minutes, jot down your first thoughts related to the three topics that form Positive Evaluation #1 through #3.

How does the Triple Positive Evaluation help you? First, you empower yourself by seeing your actual progress. You overcome an unfortunate habit that many of us have: the tendency to obsess over one detail and miss the rest of the picture. You CAN make each marketing campaign a pillar of your ongoing education in real-world marketing. One of my favorite questions to ask when I interview top professionals is: "Knowing what you know now, what would you have done differently?"

Now that you have evaluated your marketing campaign and you have found "the lesson and placed it into your Next Plan," you have done something crucial. You have taken your business "by the horns," and now you're more capable to lead your team to better and better results. Good!

* * *

Having courage and evaluating your marketing campaigns is part of a proactive approach to your small business. Now, Judi Moreo provides more strategies as she introduces us to "conscious leadership."

Conscious Leadership, Rising Profits
by Judi Moreo

Creativity is a key component in the survival of a small business today. You, as the leader, must demonstrate to your team members every day of every month of every year,

year after year, what creativity means and how important it is to your organization. Being a small business person is not easy.

You may not have the resources or the circumstances you believe you need, so start with what you have and build a foundation which will allow you to find the resources and create the circumstances you desire.

The extensive changes we are currently experiencing throughout the globe are going to demand a particular style of leadership so utterly revolutionary that it will challenge any and all existing paradigms. New thinking must become the norm in any organization where high quality and effective leadership will be the competitive edge. It must supersede outdated and obsolete management paradigms. When there is truly effective leadership, team members are mobilized to be and do their very best. It is the catalyst for transforming the organization and galvanizing everyone toward a common purpose. If you are to become this type of a leader, perhaps you will need to make some changes.

Give up blame

Blame shifts the responsibility from us to others. We think, "It's their fault." "They didn't do what they were supposed to do." "They didn't hold up their end of the bargain." "It costs too much." "They talked me into it or out of it." "They prevented me from doing what I wanted to do." The truth is it is your responsibility. Maybe you didn't do enough research or you did it because you didn't think about the consequences. Or maybe you chose to buy something you couldn't afford, instead of sticking to the budget. Perhaps you were avoiding an argument or you were scared of the alternative. Whatever the reason, your business is your responsibility.

Stop making excuses

Making excuses is another way we shift responsibility. Instead of blaming people, we blame things or circumstances. "I didn't get it done because the copy machine was broken," or "I couldn't get the repair man out here to look at the machine until next week." Perhaps you could have taken it to a local print shop to have it copied. My business partner was working on an important project when her copier broke. It was late in the evening and there were no print shops open in the small town where she lived. She called the printer at home and explained her situation to him. He volunteered to come in very early the next morning so she could get her work done in time to meet her deadline. I asked her what she would have done if the printer hadn't agreed to come. She answered, "Then I would have driven 85 miles to the next town where there is a 24-hour copy store near the university and I would have gotten it done there." Where there is a will, there is a way.

Learn to live in the present

Instead of being passive, do something. The present is the only time we have. Think to yourself, "What can I do right now to make my business the best it can be? What one step can I take to advance in a forward direction?" Start by doing the best you can wherever you are and at whatever you are doing. Years ago, there was a TV commercial that said, "If you had to sign your name to everything you did, would you do it better?" That statement really made an impact on me. Other people observe how you do things. When they see you doing your best, even when you are doing a job you don't like, they'll recognize your commitment to doing a job well and opportunities will start to present themselves. By doing your best at whatever you are doing, you are taking control of the situation.

Become a problem-solver

It is absolutely essential we become problem-solvers. Problem identifiers are a dime a dozen. Anyone can go around pointing out problems. On the other hand, problem-solvers are worth their weight in gold. Far too few people spend their time and use their minds looking for solutions. Problems give us opportunities to be creative. If you can identify a problem, you can certainly use your creative abilities to come up with a possible solution or two.

Don't confuse problem-solving with decision-making. Problem-solving is a brainstorming activity where we look at all the possible options available to us to solve a problem. Decision-making is where we select one of those possibilities. Never make a decision that is not in everyone's best interest. Make your decisions based on what you know is the right thing to do. Be sure what you choose passes the test of your conscience as well as your integrity.

When you see a problem, prepare a careful analysis of that problem and any other problems it may cause. Make sure you are looking at the real problem and not a symptom of a problem. Once you are positive you are addressing the real problem, create a list of possible solutions and recommendations for alternatives. Then evaluate each option to be sure you are doing what is right for all concerned. If you feel in your heart it is the right thing to do, do it! Remember, if you don't have problems, you aren't growing! Growth is always a creator of problems. These problems are opportunities. A problem just might be the push you need to do something differently.

Make every moment count

Like so many other people, you probably feel your life is moving faster and faster. Today we do everything fast: talk fast, drive fast, even eat fast. Time is at a premium and most of us are afflicted with "hurry sickness." There never seems to be enough time to do the things we have to do, much less those things we'd like to do. Many of us don't even have time to think. Something is terribly wrong with this picture. There are probably times when you feel like a spectator who is watching your own life unfold, instead of being in control. You might even be wondering who you are and what your purpose is!

Time is the most precious and limited resource we have. In spite of our best efforts, time is unyielding. No one can stop it, slow it down, or save it. It is a rare person who has enough time to do all the things he or she wants to do. If you are like most people, trying to balance a busy professional life and a busy personal life, you know what a challenge it can be to get everything done. Keeping current with what's going on in the world, not to mention technology, your industry, changing expectations, and personal obligations, is becoming harder and harder. For some reason, we keep adding "just one more thing," and forget to eliminate another. The result is an ever-increasing time crunch. Here are some questions for you to consider: "Do I take on too much? Do I have difficulty saying 'No' to extra demands? Do I fail to set priorities? Do I fail to plan?" Sit back, shut out your other thoughts, and imagine what it would be like to spend your time doing the things which are most important to you. Imagine using your work time on activities that directly relate to achieving your most important goals and to those tasks which must be accomplished and using your personal time to enjoy the things you really want to do.

Create a picture in your mind. Envision yourself going through the day doing work that truly makes a difference. It feels good, doesn't it?

Now that you've spent some time exercising your imagination, let's get real. We still have the same amount of time we have always had. The clock still ticks off 24 hours every day. The calendar still has seven days a week, 52 weeks a year. So why do we feel like we are running out of time? Technology has reshaped the way we work, eat, sleep, play, and live. We are living in an age of instant everything. Information is transmitted at the speed of light and is received instantly. Replies are expected immediately. It seems there is far too much to do and far too little time. You may be asking yourself on a regular basis, "How can I get all this done in the time I have?" or, "Is this all there is to life?" It's possible you are feeling less and less satisfaction, as well as more and more stress. People in this predicament often say, "I need to manage my time more effectively." or "I need to get control of my time." Realize this! You can't manage or control time. No one can. You can only manage yourself and your activities within the time you have.

People who are in positions of power are usually excellent self-managers. They have learned to set priorities, delegate effectively, and make decisions quickly, all of which are parts of managing themselves. If you want to dramatically improve the overall quality of your life, you must learn to manage yourself. Joan Baez once said, "You don't get to choose how you are going to die or when. You can only decide how you're going to live." Decide right now that you are going to start making every moment of your life count. To my knowledge, this is the only life you are going to get, so make it enjoyable, satisfying, and rewarding. There are three primary aspects to doing this: take control, work smarter, and take action.

Step #1 Take control

Taking control begins with analyzing what really happens to your time. Keep a time log for a period of two weeks in order to see exactly what you do with your time. Make a thorough analysis. When you do this, it will identify time-wasters and all activities that are not necessary, as well as where you are spending time that doesn't contribute to your goals. You will, of course, also identify time spent on areas that are getting the best results. You are probably thinking, "I don't have time to keep a time log. That's just one more thing that will add stress to my life." Stop it. That is negative. Just do it! In two weeks, you'll be glad you did, as you will no doubt be amazed at what you discover!

Step #2 Work smarter

Make a time log with six columns. Title these six columns: Time, Activity, Value, Urgent, Scheduled, and Interruption. Every half hour, write in the time and then enter what you have just done in the Activity column. In the Value column, which determines whether or not a particular activity contributes to your established goals, indicate the value by entering a plus sign which means yes, it is of value, or a minus sign which means no, it's not. Then place a check mark in the Urgent column if there is any follow-up activity that has an upcoming deadline. Make a check mark in the Scheduled column if the activity was pre-planned. Place a check mark in the Interruption column if this activity was an unexpected interruption.

You will realize from keeping this time log that there are an enormous number of activities which are not contributing to the achievement of your goals. By the time you have made a thorough analysis of everything you do, you will decide to do more of some activities and less of others. You will probably even stop doing certain activities entirely and start doing others.

After two weeks, make an in-depth analysis of your time log. This involves looking at each column and asking yourself various questions:

1. Activity column Which activities can be simplified? Which ones can be delegated or even eliminated? Which ones need more attention? Which ones were enjoyable?

2. Value column What percentage of your activities were of value?

3. Urgent column What percentage were really urgent? Were they also important? What percentage could have been taken care of sooner so they could have avoided becoming urgent?

4. Scheduled column What percentage were planned or expected?

5. Interruption column What percentage were interruptions? Who or what was your most frequent interrupter? How were you interrupted most often — phone, email, or in person? Were they necessary interruptions? Were you comfortable with how you handled them? Are there major differences between what you hoped to accomplish and what you actually did achieve? Are you spending your time pursuing those things that have high value to you? If not, why not?

Plan yearly, quarterly, monthly, weekly, and daily. The secret to successful planning is to allow extra time for unexpected situations and not over-commit or over-book. Establish priorities for your activities so that at the end of the day, you will have completed the most important things. Planning long projects and breaking them down into smaller projects and timetables will help you dedicate a few minutes each day to important high-value activities that carry future due dates. By getting ahead on projects, you are less likely to have last-minute crises and time crunches.

The following five questions will help improve your time utilization:

1. Did my activity relate directly to one or more of my goals or objectives?
2. How can my activities be better handled in the future?
3. What activities can I delegate in the future and to whom?
4. What activities will I eliminate because they are useless?
5. Which activities can I minimize or control the time involvement?

Beware of bad habits that sabotage your best efforts. Subconscious patterns can make you your own worst enemy. Whether it is trying to remember everything instead of making lists, being consistently late because you wanted to do just one more thing before leaving the office, or being easily distracted, you can change your habits. A lot of people believe they can multi-task. Actually, what people are doing is interrupting one task with another. It is nearly impossible to do things well when you are trying to do many things at the same time.

Once you have all of the available facts, make a decision. Rarely does delay improve the quality of choice. Over analysis can be seductive and stress-producing. Keep in mind that nearly all decisions must be made with imperfect information. That's why it is called a "decision." If you make a decision and you don't get the outcome you want, don't beat yourself up. Realize that you have found one more way that doesn't work and make another decision. Just keep adjusting until you do get the outcome you want.

In his book, *Think and Grow Rich,* Napoleon Hill wrote "Analysis of over 25,000 men and women who had experienced failure disclosed the fact that lack of decision-making was near the head of the list of the thirty-one major causes of failure. Procrastination, the opposite of decision, is a common enemy which practically everyone must conquer."

Step #3 Take action

Oliver Wendell Holmes said, "I find the great thing in this world is not so much where we stand as in what direction we are moving. To reach the port of Heaven, we must sail sometimes with the wind and sometimes against it, but we must sail and not drift nor lie at anchor." Action is our only choice. Without it, we become stagnant and like a ship at anchor, we'll go nowhere. We must take specific, directed action to reach our destination.

Develop your skills

Learn as much as you can about whatever it is you decide to do. Educate yourself. If you can't afford or you don't have time for a formal education, read books. Libraries are full of them and it doesn't cost you anything to go there and read or to check them out and take them home. The Internet is a very useful tool.

Nearly everything you could possibly want to know can be found on the Internet. If you don't know how, immediately learn to use it. Continue gathering knowledge and information throughout your life. Every day you are either getting better or you are getting worse. Nothing stays the same. The world is constantly evolving. You must do the same.

Pace yourself

Have you ever watched a mountain goat climb a mountain? At one time, I lived in the mountains and it was a wonderful experience to watch one of our bighorn sheep as it climbed up a mountain. He would climb for a while and when he reached a ledge, he rested. He'd look around, walk around the mountain at the same level for a while and then start to climb again, but not straight up. He went at an angle, working his way around the rocks and the brush. Sometimes, he came back down a bit, went across and started up again, stopping along the way to graze or rest. We can learn a lot from the bighorn. If we want to reach our goal, we need to stop every now and then to look around, check out where we are, where the path is taking us, and see if there are any obstacles we are going to need to go around. It may be longer to go around, but perhaps the benefits of that path are better. Sometimes we may have to go back down a bit in order to take a different path which will take us closer to our goal. Most of us don't like to backtrack, but it can be a necessary step in accomplishing our goals. We need to nurture ourselves, rest when we are tired, and pace ourselves. Otherwise, we may burn out along the way.

Commitment

Your goals have more chance of becoming a reality when you are committed to them. Many people talk about how committed they are, but when push comes to shove, they quit. Real commitment means you don't give up until you achieve the desired result. Find out the risks and rewards before you decide to follow a path. Even when an obstacle gets in your way or you have a setback, never give up.

Committed people understand there is a price to pay to achieve anything worthwhile.

The potential for greatness and innovation in your organization already exists. It's up to you to recognize, retrieve, and redeem this competitive capital. The answer lies in uniting your team and being able to create an environment that is conducive to creativity.

Judi Moreo, CSP, has presented keynote speeches, workshops, and seminars in twenty-seven countries on four continents. She is an accomplished author with nine books to her credit including *Conquer the Brain Drain: 52 Creative Ways to Pump Up Productivity, Ignite the Spark: 52 Creative Ways To Boost Creativity, Delivering Exceptional Customer Service .... a handbook for the Customer Service Person Working At The Front Line,* and her bestselling, *You Are More Than Enough* and its companion, *Achievement Journal.*

Moreo was a senior executive in a major media group in South Africa during the end of the apartheid era. Prior to taking the position in South Africa, she was a highly successful entrepreneur. The Las Vegas Chamber of Commerce honored her as a "Woman of Achievement–Entrepreneur" and upon her return to the United States, Moreo founded Turning Point International, a training and development company with offices in Las Vegas, Nevada and Johannesburg, South Africa. The US Business Advisory Council recently named her "Nevada Business Person of the Year."

Judi Moreo, CSP
P. O. Box 231360, Las Vegas, Nevada 89105, (702) 896-2228
www.judimoreo.com www.youaremorethanenough.com
www.lifechoicesbook.com

* * *

Take a moment and evaluate your own form of time management. Do you lose time when you would be better off making marketing phone calls? Do you say "yes" too easily? Now, Stephanie Marie Beeby shares with us how to "say 'no' with grace."

Saying 'No' With Grace
by Stephanie Beeby

A strong theme I have recognized in entrepreneurs around me, mostly women, is this inability to say 'no' gracefully. It is like we are in the habit of saying 'yes' so much that we can forget when to set those boundaries and to be more clear on what it is that we are really, really, really wanting.

What I have observed even in my own life is that in some ways saying 'No' was like I was declining the value of the opportunity or person, when I made a SHIFT to see that saying 'No' was actually honoring when it wasn't the ideal fit, I realized I would be doing a dis-service to say 'Yes.'

Boundary setting is a GIFT and it creates a way for us to understand what we are meant to hold space for and what we are meant to support from a distance. I have found as an entrepreneur that this skill is one of the most valuable as we move forward in our business. When we are able to make certain aspects a priority over others and give our attention there it is extremely valuable for us to learn and allow this to lead the way in determining when to partner, what to support, what to show up for and what clients to take on.

This ability to say 'No with Grace' requires us to:

- KNOW WHAT WE REALLY WANT, which means we have to choose and be clear with what is possible.
- It calls us to RAISE our level of Self-Integrity and so we know when we put our words on something that it ACTUALLY matters.
- It creates the opportunity for us to truly STAND

for what MATTERS to us and to work with those we are TRULY CALLED to do so.

- It requires us to know that we can't be everything to everyone.
- It allows us to release the 'shoulds' or 'have tos' in the process.
- It allows us to create the PRIORITIES in our life.
- It creates the space to TRULY say YES to what resonates with us.

You might be asking, **what is the difference between saying 'no' and saying 'no with grace'???**

Well, I am glad you asked. Saying 'No with Grace' requires us to know our position and the 'why' behind our choice. The Grace comes from holding and honoring the other as perfect for where they are and still knowing that we are not being called to support it in a particular way. The Grace is in the delivery of the message.... and the 'No' comes from knowing what you are truly wanting and choosing it with every decision you make. It is the process of not seeing the 'No' as judgment or needing to find fault in the other, but simply being clear of who you are, what you want and knowing when something is not resonating with that aligned message. Knowing that the timing isn't right, or that you have too much on your plate to show up fully.

My hope in writing this article is that YOU will be able to identify what matters. That YOU will create the space for you to say 'No with Grace' from a place of complete power and love. That YOU are inspired by this and evaluate all that you are saying yes to now and see if something is really meant to be a 'no.'

May YOU give yourself the permission to say 'No with Grace.'

Stephanie Beeby, Ph.D. Cand. is an Intuitive Business Strategist and expert in Intuitive Strategizing and Decision-Making for Visionary Business Owners. Trained in Organizational Psychology, she is the Founder of 'In Flow CEO' and currently assists women entrepreneurs to Clarify, Energize and Optimize their business and life systems. For more information, visit www.InFlowCEO.com and to receive a Free Report on Developing Self-Trust as well as weekly Daily GEMS right to your inbox simply register at www.StephanieBeeby.com.

* * *

As we approach the final pages of this book, I want to share with you another facet of marketing.

Can Marketing Be Spiritual?

One of my friends appears to have frequent good luck. People call him with new opportunities. New clients arrive by referral. There's something in particular that I notice: he is always helping someone.

During a recent conversation, I learned that he was looking at a stranger's resume at 1:43 AM. He did some work for this stranger by using Google.com to look up a couple of resources. My friend replied via email to the stranger with the links he found.

What's going on here? My friend is always seeking to serve. For some things he gets paid. For other things, it's just his way of flowing with each day.

Can marketing be spiritual? Yes! My friend is an example of seeking to make a contribution. Similarly, I have focused on my personal mission as "I help people experience enthusiasm, love and wisdom to fulfill big dreams."

My company also has a mission:

We create encouraging, energizing edutainment for our good and humankind's rise.
- Tom Marcoux Media, LLC Mission Caption

Every effort that my team members and I do for marketing is dedicated to a higher cause—"to serve humankind's rise."

So yes!—marketing can be spiritual.

And now I ask you: What good are you doing with your marketing efforts? How will your clients benefit from your product or service? This is where you start.

* * *

Positively evaluating your marketing campaign is crucial for your doing better with each subsequent campaign. Use the methods of this chapter to empower yourself.

Points to Remember:

*** Secret #10: Many people fail to evaluate the results of a marketing campaign.**

*** Your Countermeasure:**

Take charge of your business career. Implement the Triple Positive Evaluation. Use these steps:

Step One (Positive Evaluation #1): Identify your goals on three levels.

Step Two (Positive Evaluation #2): Find some way to praise yourself.

Step Three (Positive Evaluation #3): Find the Lesson and Place It into Your "Next Time Plan."

* * * * * *

A Final Word and Springboard to Your Success

As we come to the end of this book, I would like to take this final opportunity to discuss a few more details with you. I'm inspired to share material that I expressed on my blog: www.BeHeardandBeTrusted.com.

Have you ever flinched about having to sell something? Was it your product or your car or something else?

Some of us find selling to be such a problem that we proclaim, "I don't like to sell."

I can feel the pain of well-meaning, dedicated professionals when they cringe about marketing (and selling). These people often fail to get out the word about their product and service. The pressure they endure hurts them and their families.

If you own your business, you're not just a product or content creator. To succeed, you need to realize that you're the chief advocate and voice of your product or service.

Here I'll provide powerful methods that my clients have found valuable. I call them the Five Forward Steps:

1. Coach to Action
2. Set Effort-Goals and Result-Goals
3. Make it a game you can win
4. Keep Score and Achieve More
5. Use your "for the team" tendency

1. Coach to Action

Some people hesitate about marketing. They see it as pushing people. No! That's not it. The process is for you to be a "coach to action." What does a coach for an Olympic athlete do? He or she guides the athlete to do what's necessary to win gold.

Think of marketing your product in this way: "always be helpful." You're in the business of finding the right fit. You find the customer that can truly benefit from your product or service. You help that customer see the value of what you're offering. And you coach that customer to get involved with your product or service. Finally, if what you offer can't help the customer, you see if he or she will refer you to someone who is a good match for your product or service.

2. Set Effort-Goals and Result-Goals

Some people get stuck and their morale hits bottom. Why? Often it's because they have not separated Effort-Goals from Result-Goals. Let's say you decide to make ten prospecting calls a day. That's an Effort-Goal. Then, from those calls, your aim is to set four appointments. That's a Result-Goal.

We don't control results. We *influence* them. For example, you could call ten people and only get voicemail. No appointments have been set. Perhaps you didn't know about the industry conference that pulled all ten people out of the office. You can be proud of your success when you set and meet your Effort-Goals.

3. Make it a game you can win

Do you need to make marketing calls? Then avoid starting with a goal of 200 calls in a day. Build up to it. Start with five calls and then reward yourself when you succeed. This is a process of "make it a game you can win." Particularly when you begin a new discipline, think it through. Avoid unnecessary frustration caused by a goal that's too high for your current level of experience. Start small and build up from there.

4. Keep Score and Achieve More

I find it *self-motivating* to keep score when I write a book. I record how many pages I write each day. Often we discover that many projects require us to maintain discipline, day in and day out. Without discipline, we won't hit the big peak of achievement.

The same process applies to making calls or contacting new people. When I began on Facebook, I made an Effort Goal of contacting 20 people a day. I set up a form and noted my daily progress.

5. Use your "for-the-team" tendency

Have you met a mother who won't take five minutes out of her day to quietly have coffee but will spend three hours helping her son with his homework? She is what I call a "for-the-team" person. She will do more for her family (or team) than for herself. (As a sidenote, I would advise that mother to also take care of herself. Taking breaks is a valuable habit to form.)

If you notice that you have a "for-the-team" tendency, then you can turn it to your advantage in your marketing efforts. For example, one of my clients, Mary, discovered that she was more likely to devote efforts to marketing if the process somehow benefited someone she cared about.

Mary wanted to help her friend Tara, who had been laid off from her job. So Mary hired Tara to promote her speeches to women's associations. The initial plan was for Mary to pay Tara an hourly wage to make the marketing calls for her.

But then Mary had a new idea. She would motivate herself to do the necessary follow-up calls by adding in a benefit for Tara. Tara would receive a bonus for each sale Mary closed (setting a speaking engagement). With this,

Mary had her "for-the-team" tendency kick in, which was an important motivating factor for her. And, in so doing, Mary felt accountable for something good happening to Tara.

Implement the Five Forward Steps:

1. Coach to Action
2. Set Effort-Goals and Result-Goals
3. Make it a game you can win
4. Keep Score and Achieve More
5. Use your "for-the-team" tendency

Take these steps and you'll feel great each day. You will begin see good results blossom.

Finally, I encourage you to go back to the chapters in this book and benefit from working with the *9-minute Methods*. When you use this book like a workbook, your benefits double.

It has been a joy to share my ideas with you throughout this book. I hope to work with you again, perhaps at one of my presentations or through one-to-one coaching.

Congratulations on your efforts with this book. Thank you for your attention. When you return to these pages again and again, you can *reenergize yourself*. You will get more value each time you review the steps covered in this book.

To gain more value and use this book as a springboard, be sure to go through it and note your new tasks *in your calendar*. Take some action. Any action towards improving skills and enlarging your life is helpful. I often say, "Better than zero."

* * *

Please consider gaining special training through my coaching (phone and in-person), workshops, presentations and Top Five Group Elite Video Training. My coaching features innovations: *Dynamic Rehearsal* and *Power Rehearsal for Crisis*. Due to my background in improvisation and training in acting, directing and screenwriting, I help clients *as I improvise dialogue* during rehearsal sessions. I coach clients to prepare for speeches and any tough or vital conversation with audiences, colleagues, sales prospects and even family members.

As you continue to work toward expanding your financial abundance and fulfillment in life, you are likely to come up against some tough situations. To be supportive I've written a number of books . . .

- Darkest Secrets of Charisma
- Darkest Secrets of Persuasion and Seduction Masters: How to Protect Yourself and Turn the Power to Good
- Darkest Secrets of Negotiation Masters
- Darkest Secrets of Making a Pitch to the Film and Television Industry
- Darkest Secrets of Film Directing
- Darkest Secrets of the Film and Television Industry Every Actor Should Know
- Darkest Secrets of Spiritual Seduction Masters
- Power Time Management: More Time, Less Stress and Zero Procrastination

See my blog at
www.BeHeardandBeTrusted.com

The best to you,
Tom
Tom Marcoux,

America's Communication Coach, TFG Thought Leader, Motion Picture Director, Actor, Producer, Screenwriter
P.S. See **Free Chapters** of Tom Marcoux's 25 books at http://amzn.to/ZiCTRj (at Amazon.com)

Titles include:
Be Heard and Be Trusted
Nothing Can Stop You This Year
Truth No One Will Tell You
Yes! Secrets for Your Best Life . . . Law of Attraction . . .
Reduce Clutter, Enlarge Your Life
Wake Up Your Spirit to Prosperity — and more.
(For coaching, reach Tom Marcoux at tomsupercoach@gmail.com)

EXCERPT FROM
DARKEST SECRETS OF PERSUASION AND SEDUCTION MASTERS: HOW TO PROTECT YOURSELF AND TURN THE POWER TO GOOD

by Tom Marcoux, America's Communication Coach
Copyright Tom Marcoux

. . . Now, I am in my 40's, with gray in my hair, and for 27 years I have been taking action to protect people.

And now is the time for me to protect you with the Countermeasures I reveal in this book.

Every human being needs to be able to
break the trance that a Manipulator creates.
You need to make good decisions
so you are safe and you keep growing
—and you are not cut down and crippled.

This Darkest Secrets material is so intense that I first

released it only with the counterbalance of my most energizing and uplifting books, *Nothing Can Stop You This Year!* and *10 Seconds to Wealth: Master the Moment Using Your Divine Gifts.*

An interviewer asked me: "Who can be the Manipulator?"

A co-worker, a boss, a salesperson, someone you're dating, and someone you think is a friend.

Now is the time—this very minute—for me to write this book to protect you.

I must speak the truth.

These Darkest Secrets of "persuasion masters" are ...

Wait a minute! Let's say it plainly: These are the Darkest Secrets of masters of manipulation. Throughout this book, I will call these people what they are: Manipulators.

Dictionary.com defines "manipulate" as "To influence or manage shrewdly or deviously.... To tamper with or falsify for personal gain."

In this book, we will look on a manipulator as one who deviously influences someone with no concern about that person's well-being, and who causes harm to that person.

Here is the first Darkest Secret:

Darkest Secret #1:
Manipulators Make You Hurt
and Then Offer the Salve.

Manipulators would invite you to go out in the sun for hours and then sell you the salve to soothe your burns. The problem is that we don't notice that this is what they're doing.

For example, you're considering the purchase of a house. A Manipulator asks the question, "So, where would you put your TV?" This question is designed to put you into a trance.

Dictionary.com defines "trance" as "a half-conscious state, seemingly between sleeping and waking, in which ability to function voluntarily may be suspended." Let's condense this: in a trance you may not be able to function freely.

Here is the second Secret:

Darkest Secret #2:

Manipulators Put You into a Trance.

To protect yourself, you must learn to use Countermeasures to Break the Trance.

All the Countermeasures (actions you can take to break the trance) in this book will make you stronger and more capable of protecting yourself.

Now, we'll view the third Secret:

Darkest Secret #3:

Manipulators Care Nothing for You and Human Decency: They'll lie, cheat, and do whatever they need to do so they win—but their charm masks all this.

Let's return to the example of a Manipulator selling you a house. A Manipulator does not pause for an instant to see if you can truly afford the new house. The Manipulator would neglect to mention that you will not only have your mortgage payment of $900. There will be additional costs: home repairs, property tax, water, electricity, homeowner's insurance, and more. The Manipulator only emphasizes what he or she knows you want to hear: "Look! $900 is better than the $1500 you're paying for rent, which is just going down the toilet. And the $900 is an investment."

Let's go back to **Darkest Secret #1:**

Manipulators make you hurt and then offer the salve.

The Manipulator has you feeling good about the solution (salve) and feeling bad about your current life situation.

How? A Manipulator will make you hurt through questions such as:

- What bothers you about paying $1500 a month for rent?

(The Manipulator will use a derisive tone when he says the word rent.)

• What is not smart about paying rent on someone else's house instead of investing in your own house?

• How do you feel about your children walking in the neighborhood where you live now?

Do you see how these questions are designed to make you hurt enough so that you'll buy?

An interviewer asked me, "Tom, aren't these good arguments for purchasing a house?"

"What we're looking at is the *intention* of the influencer," I replied. "Let's look at our definition of a manipulator as one who deviously influences someone with no concern about that person's well-being, and who causes harm to that person. If the person truly cannot afford the house, he or she will be harmed by buying it. If the manipulator conceals the truth, the manipulator is doing harm. That's the important difference."

Some friends of mine are ethical and helpful real estate agents who truthfully reveal the whole situation and help the purchaser achieve her own goals.

In this book, we are talking about another type of person; that is, unethical Manipulators.

* * *

In any given moment, we need to remember the tactics Manipulators use. We will focus on the word D.A.R.K. so you can remember details easily and protect yourself from Manipulators.

D — Dangle something for nothing

A — Alert to scarcity

R — Reveal the Desperate Hot Button

K — Keep on pushing buttons

1. Dangle Something for Nothing

What do conmen and conwomen do to seize your attention? They make you think you're getting a "steal."

I recently saw a documentary in which a conman on a street in England showed a toy that looked like it was dancing. This fake product was actually dancing because of a hidden, invisible thread. The conman was dangling something for nothing. The Entranced Buyer thought he was getting something worth $20 for only $5. That was the trick. The Entranced Buyer felt that he was getting $15 extra of value for his $5. What the Buyer really got was something worth nothing. Similarly, I know someone who purchased a copy of a Disney movie from a street vendor in San Francisco. She brought the copy home and it was unwatchable—and the street vendor was never seen again.

An old phrase goes, "A conman cannot con someone who is not looking for something for nothing."

How to Protect Yourself from "Dangle Something for Nothing"

Stop! Get on your cell phone and talk through the "deal" with someone you know who thinks clearly. Go home. Think about it. Do some research on the Internet. Listen to your gut feelings. If the salesman or conman is too insistent, get away from that Manipulator. Get quiet. Have a cup of water. Cool down. Break the Trance!

Break the Trance and Identify the Crucial Detail

Earlier, I mentioned that a Manipulator puts you into a trance. An added problem is that we put ourselves into a trance. For example, as you read this, are you thinking about your right toe? Most likely not (unless you stubbed your toe recently). The point is that we only focus on a tiny percentage of what is going on in our life.

Around fifteen years ago, I caused myself trouble because I put myself into a trance. I discovered that under certain conditions, friendship can make you nearly deaf. Here's how: I was producing a song for a motion picture. A good friend was singing backup in the chorus. Because of our friendship, I wanted him to sound great. I completely missed the Crucial Detail. In this kind of situation, the Crucial Detail is that what truly counts is how the lead singer sounds! I made a song that I could not release. What a waste of time and money! I had put myself into a trance.

In any situation in which the Manipulator is "dangling something for nothing," we often fall into a trance and miss the Crucial Detail. The most important detail is *not* that we're saving money if we order before midnight tonight. What counts is whether the product creates a lasting, crucial benefit in our lives. And is the benefit of the product worth the cost? Some people even program themselves to make mistakes by saying, "I can't pass up a bargain." The bargain is *not* the Crucial Detail.

Secrets to Break the Trance

This is the process of B.R.E.A.K.S. It will help you remember the proven methods to break a trance.

End of Excerpt from
DARKEST SECRETS OF PERSUASION AND SEDUCTION MASTERS: HOW TO PROTECT YOURSELF AND TURN THE POWER TO GOOD

Purchase your copy of this book (paperback or ebook) at Amazon.com or BarnesandNoble.com
See **Free Chapters** of Tom Marcoux's 25 books at http://amzn.to/ZiCTRj

ABOUT THE AUTHOR

Tom Marcoux helps people like you fulfill big dreams. Known as America's Communication Coach and TFG Thought Leader, Tom has authored 24 books with sales in 15 countries. One of his *Darkest Secrets* books rose to #1 on Amazon.com Hot New Releases in Business Life (and in Business Communication). He guides clients and audiences (IBM, Sun Microsystems, etc.) to success in job interviewing, public speaking, media relations, and branding. A member of the National Speakers Association, he is a professional coach and guest expert on TV, radio, and print, and was dubbed "the Personal Branding Instructor" by the *San Francisco Examiner.*

Tom addressed National Association of Broadcasters' Conference six years running. With a degree in psychology, Tom is a guest lecturer at **Stanford University**, DeAnza, & California State University, and teaches public speaking, science fiction cinema/literature and comparative religion at Academy of Art University. Winner of a special award at the **Emmys**, Tom wrote, directed, and produced a feature film that the distributor took to the **Cannes film market**, and the film gained international distribution. He is engaged in book/film projects *Crystal Pegasus* (children's) and *TimePulse* (science fiction). See TomSuperCoach.com and Tom's well-received blog at www.BeHeardandBeTrusted.com

Tom Marcoux can help you with **speech writing** and

coaching for your best performance.

As Tom says, *Make Your Speech a Pleasant Beach.*

Join Tom's Linkedin.com group: *Executive Public Speaking and Communication Power.*

At Google+: join the community "Create Your Best Life – Charisma & Confidence"

Get a **Free** report: "9 Deadly Mistakes to Avoid for Your Next Speech and 9 Surefire Methods" at

http://tomsupercoach.com/freereport9Mistakes4Speech.html

Tom Marcoux has trained CEOs, small business owners, and graduate students to speak with impact and gain audiences' tremendous approval and cooperation. *Learn how to present and get thunderous applause!*

"Tom, Thanks for your coaching and work with me on revising my speech at a major university. Working with you has been so enlightening for me. Through your gentle prodding and guidance I was able to write a speech that connects with the audience. I wish everyone could experience the transformation I have undergone. You have helped me discover the warm and compelling stories that now make my speech reach hearts and uplift minds. This was truly an empowering experience. I cannot thank you enough for your great assistance." — J.S.

"Tom Marcoux has been an NAB Conference favorite [speaker] for six years. And he is very energetic."

– John Marino,
Vice President, National Association of Broadcasters,
Washington, D.C.

"Using just one of Tom Marcoux's methods, I got more done in 2 weeks than in 6 months."

– Jaclyn Freitas, M.A.

Tom's Coaching features innovations:

- Dynamic Rehearsal
- Power Rehearsal for Crisis
- The Charisma Advantage that Saves Time

Become a fan of Tom's graphic novels/feature films:
Fantasy Thriller: *Jack AngelSword*
type "JackAngelSword" at Facebook.com

Science fiction: *TimePulse*
www.facebook.com/timepulsegraphicnovel

Children's Fantasy: *Crystal Pegasus*
www.facebook.com/crystalpegasusandrose

See **Free Chapters** of Tom Marcoux's 25 books
at http://amzn.to/ZiCTRj

Special Offer Just for Readers of this Book:
Contact Tom Marcoux at tomsupercoach@gmail.com for special discounts on books, coaching, workshops, special video-based training and presentations. Just mention your experience with this book.

www.ingramcontent.com/pod-product-compliance
Lightning Source LLC
Chambersburg PA
CBHW070522200326
41519CB00013B/2900
* 9 7 8 0 6 9 2 3 5 8 5 0 4 *